The date of the photo of this sunset was June 9th, 2008 which was the day that Dorothy died in Minnesota. It was taken by Cathy, my granddaughter-in-law, in Fox Lake, Illinois, without any knowledge of Dorothy's condition. Cathy was so impressed with the scene that she felt she needed to take the picture to preserve it. She was very surprised when she learned what happened that day. Dorothy loved to watch the sunsets over the lake at our Wisconsin home.

Balboa Press books may be ordered through booksellers or by contacting:

Balboa Press
A Division of Hay House
1663 Liberty Drive
Bloomington, IN 47403
www.balboapress.com
1-(877) 407-4847

Because of the dynamic nature of the Internet, any web addresses or links contained in this book may have changed since publication and may no longer be valid. The views expressed in this work are solely those of the author and do not necessarily reflect the views of the publisher, and the publisher hereby disclaims any responsibility for them.

The author of this book does not dispense medical advice or prescribe the use of any technique as a form of treatment for physical, emotional, or medical problems without the advice of a physician, either directly or indirectly. The intent of the author is only to offer information of a general nature to help you in your quest for emotional and spiritual well-being. In the event you use any of the information in this book for yourself, which is your constitutional right, the author and the publisher assume no responsibility for your actions.

Any people depicted in stock imagery provided by Thinkstock are models, and such images are being used for illustrative purposes only.
Certain stock imagery © Thinkstock.

Printed in the United States of America.

ISBN: 978-1-4525-8127-9 (sc)
ISBN: 978-1-4525-8126-2 (e)

Library of Congress Control Number: 2013915656

Balboa Press rev. date: 9/6/2013

# I Married an Angel,
## and Now She's in Heaven

A memoir with miracles, religious thoughts and prayers.

By Dr. Raymond Broz

**BALBOA.**
PRESS
A DIVISION OF HAY HOUSE

# CONTENTS

# Acknowledgements

I feel extremely fortunate to have been invited to live my son Rick and his wife Hedy. Being able to live with his whole family is really a blessing for me.

In addition Rick's company, Culinary Wizard, gave me office space which included a desk and a computer. Also available were expert instructors on the operation of a computer. They started me from ground zero to a point where I was able to do about 80% of the typing of my manuscript.

I needed to get Dorothy's life and events after her death available for others to read. She was a great and unusual person, and, to me, the events after her death are extraordinary. These spiritual events are beyond comprehension if a person does not believe in life after death.

I want to thank Rick's whole family for the help and guidance in completing this manuscript. In addition I need to thank my daughter Barbara for her assistance as well.

# Dedication

To my precious darling, *Dorothy Ann Osborn Broz*

# Prologue

This book is the first public announcement that I am making of the miraculous happenings that occurred during my wife's life including her last illness and death.

The first miracle occurred on July 6th, 2007, a year before Dorothy's death. She was ill with dementia, and she was in our apartment at the time. However a key to a pick-up truck appeared on the sand at our lake home in Wisconsin. It was a normal automobile key which was next to the left back wheel of a lady's pick-up that unlocked the passenger door that had the keys locked inside.

The second and third miracles occurred to me, after her death, again at our lake home. I was picking up split logs on July 8th, 2008, when she spoke to me while I was alone. I was working on a hot day, and she told me, "That's enough already." I could not believe it at first, and I continued to work. Now she spoke to me again, saying the same thing, "That's enough already." This time I am convinced that this is Dorothy's voice speaking to me clearly, and I immediately stopped working. She is still helping me.

Four days later, on July 12th, 2008, also at our lake home, my grandson's wife, Kate, saw my wife, Dorothy, in a dream, beautifully radiant, and Dorothy spoke to her also. She said, "Tell Paul that this place is not the same." This is the fourth miracle.

The greatest miracle of all, occurred to this same grandson, Paul and his wife, Kate who had a new born son, Atlas, who was about two months old. He was hospitalized in Children's Memorial Hospital in Chicago about December 26, 2008, because he was unable to retain his feedings. He was scheduled to have surgery on December 29th. I was informed of that on December 28th, the day before surgery, and I prayed to Dorothy to please help our baby, Atlas. He was **CURED** that day, and the surgery was **CANCELED**!! Instead of surgery, his parents were able to take him home. He has been healthy ever since. My angel, Dorothy, cured our great grandson.

Besides these events, I have had eagles flying over me on three different occasions in two different states. The first time was when I was living in Minnesota, and in addition, there were two occasions where I am living now in Illinois. The first two times it was only one eagle, and the third time, there were three eagles, single file. I have heard her voice, and she sends eagles over me. Surely she is in heaven. I keep calling her my angel, but I really believe she is my saint.

These supernatural events are so outstanding that I need to tell the whole world that Dorothy is in heaven. That our Heavenly Father had a place for her in heaven as He had promised. God is real, and Dorothy is alive. She also told me before she died that she would see me in heaven. I hope her prophesy is correct.

# Introduction

When I married Dorothy on June 9, 1945, God gave me a beautiful, precious person to have and to hold until death do us part. I am sure that He meant I should protect her, love her, and take care of her, until one of us has died. With that in mind, we began our marriage. We were inseparable from then on until I went into the Army in World War II. Dorothy traveled with me until I was ordered to go over seas. So for fourteen months, including the birth of our first child, we were separated. When I returned, we were together from then on. One friend called us "love birds" because I appeared to be hovering over her all the time.

She was my precious jewel that I loved and cherished her every day. We had eight wonderful children, and she had everything, mink coats, cars, vacations. Our children never saw us argue or scream at each other because we never did. I tried very hard to please her, and she knew it. In every life, a little rain must fall, but mine was a thunder storm. In reading this book, you will laugh and perhaps cry, but it contains more joy than tears, and our marriage was so great, that I wanted to share it with you.

At the end of my memoir, I have added a quasi religious section which I feel needs to be repeated and studied again as we get older and circumstances change. We need to refresh and renew our spiritual life as we go year after year. Personally I have used religion as my avocation almost all my life. It actually dove-tailed well with my medical practice.

# Chapter 1: Courtship

I was attending Mass one Sunday, and the reading for that day was about giving to Caesar what is Caesar's and giving to God what is God's. In all my years, I have heard that many times, and many of you know it well. However, in the homily, the priest repeated, "And you have to give God what is God's."

On the way home I kept thinking about this and was suddenly struck by this thought. My wife had died six months ago on our sixty-third wedding anniversary. God had given me Dorothy in marriage, and I had given her back to Him sixty-three years later. She had been very ill and she had asked me to let her go. With great sadness in my heart, I told the doctor in the emergency room to please make her comfortable. She died an hour later.

From the very start of our marriage, there was no doubt in my mind that our union had to last. In our families, the vows we had spoken at the altar were permanent. My parents had almost reached their seventieth anniversary, and Dorothy's parents were close to their fiftieth. Our goal was to stay together to the end, with never a thought of separation.

My story actually begins when I graduated from medical school on December 18, 1943. This was during World War II, and we were on an accelerated program. Originally, we were to be the class of 1944.

There was a quota on hospitals as to how many interns they could accept. Oak Park Hospital in Oak Park, Illinois would be the third hospital I applied to. This hospital was a Catholic hospital run by nuns. There was no time for mailing an application, so I decided to go there in person. Two days after Christmas, I walked up to Mother Superior's office and asked her if an internship was available. She said yes and asked when I could start. To her astonishment, I replied, "January 1st." At the time, internships had been reduced to nine months instead of twelve. Because I was in the Army, I would be leaving the hospital at the end of September.

I was unaware that this hospital also ran a nursing school, so to my surprise, I was exposed to three levels of students, freshman, juniors, and seniors. It was also my impression that the admission office's criteria included, beside grades, a certain level of beauty in the nursing students. While I was in school, including high school, I had only one date with a girl named Florence. After we got to her home, I wished her a good night and gave her a kiss. Up until that time, she was the first and only girl I had ever kissed.

However, my only goal was to become a doctor, and I had neither time nor desire to prevent me from reaching my goal. I felt that while I was in medical school, I would not have the time or the money to date any girl, no matter how beautiful, but suddenly I found myself surrounded with beautiful girls everywhere I looked. Yet for me, dating could only be a prelude to marriage, and to me marriage meant children. I was not ready for either, and I believed that there would be plenty of time to address that part of my life after I finished my medical training.

As I worked in different areas of the hospital during my internship, I observed various student nurses who were working there. At this point I felt I could be interested in finding a female partner, and I found myself looking at each girl's left hand. If I saw an engagement ring on her finger, I would stay away, not wanting perhaps to cause a break up with a GI who was in active duty. I had read enough about Dear John letters, and the sorrow those servicemen experienced. My main concern was that he might return home and shoot me or commit suicide.

Dorothy in her younger years.

After about three or four months at the hospital, the student nurses arranged a date for me with a senior student named, Alice. She and I went to a movie, and, as usual, I slept through it. I was very tired, because my work schedule did not allow for much sleep. I was able to go home every second night to be get a full night sleep. Every two days, I would get one half-day off.

After sleeping through the movie in the theater, I drove her home because I had to work in the morning. We did some kissing in the car, and it was okay at first. But then it became a bit strange. It seemed that each time we kissed, she would put her tongue out and hit my lips. I didn't know what to think of it, but she would always put her tongue out when I tried to kiss her. After a while, she said she was going in and left. We did not date again, because I felt that there was no chemistry between us. Later on I became aware of open mouth kissing.

Two months later, in early July, I received a call to go to the emergency room to tend to a student nurse who had burned her hand with hot water. When I got there, I saw the most beautiful girl that I had ever seen. I could hardly believe my eyes. I had to remain professional, because the emergency room nurse on duty was at my side. In an instant, my brain was spinning, and my heart was telling me to find out who she is. I was looking at her hand where she burned it and getting my self under control. Then I asked her what had happened. She told me that she had been sterilizing some baby bottle nipples in boiling water when some of it splashed over her hand. It was a minor burn, and I told her that she could put ice or cold water on it if it was painful. I asked her where she had been working, and she replied that she had been working in the nursery. I mentioned that I had been here for six months, and I had not seen her. She said that she had been working in a hospital in Peoria for pediatric training during that time. Incidentally, while examining her hands, I noticed that there were no rings on her fingers.

After passing her State Boards, she received her License.

Ponca City Okla.
June 4th 1944

Dear Dorothy –
        Congratulations on your Graduation, wishing you the best of everything. I looked everywhere for a suitable card, could not find one, so chose a birthday card. Am inclining a little something, perhaps you can get something you like. Hope this finds you well, we are well, Grandpa some better but has been very bad. We are having some cloudy cool days again. Vera & John were here a few min. yesterday all are well, Mamie took me to town Friday, they were all well, will close with loads of love    Grom

A note from Grandma Osborn in Ponca City, OK.

The next day, I visited the nursery to see how her hand was. She said it was fine. I also noticed that the name stitched on her uniform pocket was, "D. Osborn." Then I asked her what the "D" stood for, and she said, "Dopey." I smiled and said, "Come on, tell me." With a smile on her face, she said, " I told you. Dopey," and she turned and nonchalantly walked away. Later I learned that student nurses were forbidden to date staff doctors. I also learned that she had already graduated with the class of '44, and she just needed to finish some school time for the period she missed due to an appendectomy.

For a couple of weeks I spent most of the time asking the other nurses what her name was. They all replied, "Dopey, just like she said." Finally, one day a nurse came up to me and whispered, "Dorothy." There was a definite chemistry there. Whenever the hospital was looking for me, they would invariably call the nursery and find me there. Every free moment I could find, I would visit Dorothy in the nursery until she finally told me, " Don't just stand there, fold these diapers." At that time I did not realize that I was mesmerized by her beauty, and all I wanted was to be close by and to be watching her. However I started to fold the diapers until I was called away.

We saw each other almost every day while I was working. We became quite friendly and really got to know each other's background. However, my active duty date for the Army of October 1st was approaching. I also learned that I had the option to stay another nine months to extend my internship with the approval of the hospital administration. I was not anxious to leave for the service, so I asked Mother Superior if I could stay till July 1 of the following year. She was happy to hear that I wanted to stay, because she had only one intern coming in October. I was greatly relieved, especially having met Dorothy just six weeks ago.

About two months after we met, Dorothy told me she had plans to go to visit her grandparents for a week in Ponca City, Oklahoma. She planned to go by bus. I became immediately concerned, as traveling by bus was slow and tiresome. Also the trip would take about twenty-four hours, and that meant she would have to sleep on the bus as well. Now a young lady, traveling alone and sleeping, frightened me. But she had her tickets, and she was going. Dorothy said that she wanted to see her grand parents, because her grandmother had to provide all the care for her grandfather who was completely bed ridden. I asked her for their address, so I could write to her while she was there.

After she gave it to me, I felt somewhat relieved that I could stay in touch. I began writing a letter to her, only to realize that I had only known her for a short time. I didn't have a lot to say, but I did want to tell her that I thought of her as my sweetheart. So I wrote that down in the letter. I had been wanting to tell her that for a while, but it seemed a little awkward at the hospital where we were seeing each other. This was a good opportunity, and I felt it was more private. I was pretty sure she felt the same way. I closed the letter by asking her if she thought that was okay. I found out that I was right, and when she returned home, our romance moved to a higher level. It seemed to be true that absence makes the heart grow fonder.

Dorothy and I continued to see each other as our respective duties permitted, and we became the "Romance of Oak Park hospital." The School of Nursing rules stated that no student nurse could date a staff doctor, but again since Dorothy had already graduated, we were not breaking any rules.

There was a Dr. Ralph who was a staff doctor and a good friend of mine. He was a bit of a prankster who always wanted a little fun. He would tell Dorothy not to marry me before I left for active duty. Then he would tell me I ought to get married before I left. He was only testing us to see who would win. To complicate things, Dorothy told me that if I went on active duty before we were married, she would also enlist in the military as a nurse. I did not like that idea at all. Dr. Ralph was one of the older doctors since most of the younger doctors were in the service. He was married but had no children. Whenever he would see Dorothy or me, he would smile broadly and chuckle, finding a bit of humor in being able to give advice to a younger generation. I was aware of what he was doing, but I never said anything to him about it.

The following weeks turned into months, and my busy schedule kept me working every other night. That meant that I was on duty for sixteen straight hours. This was the time when all IVs had to be started by a doctor, so I had to stay fully dressed, except to take my shoes off for a nap. I used my father's car almost every day to go back and forth to the hospital, and, on my night off, so I could pick up Dorothy at her apartment. We would usually only go for a short ride. I was always so tired that I had to go home to get some sleep. I keep referring to the need for sleep, because the fatigue element is very important. I had to be as alert at 2pm as well as 2am to avoid any mishaps. This has always been imperative in the medical care of patients.

Dorothy's official graduation picture. Her name is on her pocket.

During the holidays I was able to meet Dorothy's family, and we would have an occasional meal together. During our short rides, we would talk and do some kissing, and then I had to get home because I was on duty at 7 AM the next day. Now I had been on this schedule for a full year in December, and I felt that we knew each other well enough to get married. I thought of an engagement ring for Christmas, but I did not want a long engagement. I had to work for six additional months at the hospital on this crazy schedule, so I bought Dorothy a large stuffed animal instead. I could see that she was disappointed, but she smiled and seemed happy. In my mind, an engagement was a very serious step, and I did not want to give her an engagement ring until we were ready.

My first enlistment while I was in Medical School. I was a Pfc for 6 months.

Spring came quickly, and I thought we should go on an official date. I had taken up golf in junior college, and my brother had a set of clubs. So on a warm and pleasant afternoon we went to the Hillside Golf Course, and I gave Dorothy a few instructions on the basics. She learned very quickly, and we proceeded to play our first round of golf at the Hillside Golf Course. This was close to Dorothy's home, so we didn't need to do a lot of traveling. This was wartime, and gasoline was being rationed.

Finally I decided to give Dorothy an engagement ring at Easter Time. One of the staff doctors suggested that I should go to his jeweler friend who could give me a choice of diamonds. Dorothy already told me she preferred white gold for jewelry, and she also gave me her ring size. I had to make a trip downtown to Chicago to see this jeweler. When I got there, his office had a special door with a window in it. You had to identify yourself before they let you in. Then he brought out a tray of diamonds of various sizes and cuts and prices. After I picked out the diamond, he said he could mount it in a white gold band. I picked it up one week later. That Easter Sunday I gave her the ring without any fanfare except for a long, "I love you" kiss. She was thrilled, excited, and delighted, all at the same time.

Then she told me that she did have an engagement ring from another man, but she had never worn it. After she met me, she tried to return it to him, but he refused to take it back. So she ended up throwing it at him, and it fell to the ground. He told her that he wanted to marry her. She answered that she never intended to marry him, and she turned and walked away. She told me that he was not her type.

With our engagement in place, we set our wedding date for June 9, 1945. The plan was that I would leave the hospital on June 1st and then I would be leaving for active duty about July 1st. When Dr. Ralph heard we were getting married, he said he knew of a nice place for a honeymoon. He was very nice to us now that we were officially engaged. Remember this was still wartime, and both tires and gasoline were rationed. He said that he would be able to make reservations for us in French Lick, Indiana, a day's drive from Chicago. This was a health spa and a tourist area close to a state park which had a lake. I thought that was a good idea, and I accepted his offer. I had no opportunity to plan anything while working at the hospital.

# Chapter 2: Wedding

We finalized the remaining affairs of our wedding. Everything was set, or so we thought. We quickly learned that we had to do everything twice. Dorothy wanted a particular priest to perform the ceremony but she had to agree to be married by the pastor of Dorothy's church, who insisted on performing the wedding. The reception hall we wanted called, and said they couldn't obtain the food. The baker who was to make our cake couldn't get sugar, which was also rationed, and then the printer called and said he couldn't get the paper for the invitations.

After finding other people who could do everything we needed, Dorothy thought we were finally ready. She went to her seamstress to check on her wedding dress, only to discover that she had not even started on it. Dorothy just about had a stroke. I believe the seamstress had assumed Dorothy would be pregnant, since I was going into the Army. This is very common. Finally, the dress was ready in time, and we got married. The pastor, Father Wheal, said he would perform the wedding, even though Dorothy had wanted Father John. Father Wheal was an older priest, very meticulous when saying mass, which would make the mass extra long. I felt this would be a sign that this marriage would last. No quickie marriage here.

On our wedding day, June 9th, 1945, I was in church when I first saw Dorothy wearing a gorgeous, flowing wedding gown. I could hardly believe my eyes. She was exquisite and lovely, and she was my bride. Again my head was in a whirl, almost as though I was in a different world. She was so overwhelming. It was hard for me to believe that this was happening to me.

Later that day, my new mother-in-law asked me how I liked the music at the mass? She said she had arranged to have her special friend sing for us. I said, "What music?" I was oblivious to what was going on except that I was marrying Dorothy at the altar. Our whole wedding day started with the long mass in the morning, and the reception with dinner in the evening and then dancing afterward.

On their way to church, Dorothy and her mother, and her father is in the background.

We put our heads together and it lasted for 63 years.

Wedding Day with Grandma Bilek on my right and Grandma Broz on our left.

Our wedding day, June 9th 1945 with my new in-laws. Wonderful people.

Our wedding party Loretta, Me, Dorothy, Jeanne, and Dr. Fitz. My sister Rose put herself in.

Wedding picture with smiles including my brother Dr. Aloysius. I am the last living person.

There was an open bar, and some fellow nurses from the hospital came to the reception. We toasted with beer mugs and my stein broke, spilling beer on the floor and on our legs, causing me to smell of beer the rest of the evening. One of Dorothy's uncles came to me and said that they couldn't find Dorothy. I looked around and I could not see her anywhere. I really got frightened and didn't know what to do. I must have shown my fear, because then her uncles brought her out of a broom closet where they had hidden her!

The music started, and I was dancing and drinking beer. I am not a beer drinker but I had my share that day. I was dancing with my cousin, Agnes, while Dorothy was dancing with someone else. I told Agnes that I married an angel and asked her, "Isn't she beautiful?"

When we left the hall and I got my car, we drove one block and stopped because someone had attached tin cans on the rear bumper. This was causing a loud racket when I drove. They were wired on, and I could not tear them off. So I picked them up off the road and put them over the bumper. Then we proceeded to my home in Berwyn. When we got there, Dorothy looked around and said, "Where is your suitcase?" I told her that I didn't have one. We started looking for something my parents might have, and we found one. I put a few things in it, and we were off to our hotel in downtown Chicago.

We checked in and got into our room just as I got very nauseated. I quickly went to the bathroom and began to vomit. I was holding on to the toilet so I would not make a mess. Dorothy did not know what to think, but I told h er that it was too much beer. The next day was Sunday, and the church was close enough to walk to for Mass. However, I wanted my car, so the attendant went to get it. All of a sudden I heard the rattling cans coming down the ramp from the garage, and everyone in the garage started to laugh. Later the men in the garage were able to remove them.

We started on our way to French Lick Indiana, which was several hours drive from Chicago. We used my father's car, a 1939 Buick that he had purchased used. Shortly after we started on our way, the engine began to overheat. I stopped on the shoulder and looked under the hood. To my surprise, I saw a small stream of water leaking out of the engine. I needed to plug it up with something to save the water. I looked down on the ground near the car and I found a spent wooden kitchen matchstick. Surprisingly, it fit right into the hole and stopped the leak completely. Looking back, this was our first spiritual event, with others to follow.

We continued on our way, but soon the engine began to overheat again. I turned on the heater and opened all the windows, but that didn't work. I parked on the shoulder of the road again to let the car cool down. Then I continued to drive and stop all the way to French Lick, We arrived about 10:00 pm only to find that the rooming house was closed. However a woman in a second-floor window told us that we would have to stay in the local motel and return the next day. They also said that they did not serve meals. We were able to find and check in at the motel. Fortunately, there was a local café nearby that we had to use for our meals.

The next day we returned to the rooming house and checked in, I asked our hosts if there was a garage in town where I could have my car fixed? They said there was no garage in this town, but there was one in the next town over, Naomi, Indiana. We limped along to Naomi and found the garage. There was only one mechanic, and he said he was busy. I would have to come another day. However after pleading our case, he said he would fix our car. He discovered that the leak was in a freeze plug that could easily be replaced. However, when he looked again, he found that the radiator needed repair also. Saying that he could do it. but that it would take all day. I was very pleased that he would be able to repair it, and it could be done all in one day. So we stayed, went to a movie, and did some sightseeing. When we returned, the car was ready, and soon we were on our way with a car in much better condition No more over heating. Another spiritual happening.

The next day was beautiful and sunny, and our thoughts were to find that Indiana State park and especially the lake. So we put on our swimming suits and found the park with the lake. There was no one else around. It seemed a pity that no one else was there to enjoy this beautiful day at the lake. The sand beach was warm from the sun and the water was cool but pleasant. After a dip in the water, I laid on my abdomen to get some sun on my back.

Since it had been several years since I was exposed to that much sun, I got a terrible sunburn. When we got back to our room, Dorothy put some Noxzema cream on my back. With the first touch, I leaped as if she put a piece of ice on me. She never forgot that moment, and repeated it to others many times, saying she thought she was killing her new husband.

Our reservation was for one week, but before the end of the week Dorothy said that she wanted to go home to see her mother. We had two days left, and there were no other plans after our trip. We headed back to Berwyn and checked in at the hotel. My parents invited us to stay with them the next day which we agreed to, because my military orders would be coming to their address anyway.

# Chapter 3: Military Service

My orders came, and I was to report for active duty at Carlisle Barracks, PA, on July 5th for officer's basic training. Wives could accompany their husbands to the base, but only for two days. So we purchased two railroad tickets to go to Harrisburg from Chicago and then we took the bus to Carlisle. After the two days were up, Dorothy stayed at the Penn-Harris Hotel in Harrisburg and took the bus to visit me. She was able to stay there for a military rate of $3.00 a day.

One of my classmates from medical school, Dr. Ted and his wife with their two children, were able to rent a home in Carlisle. He invited us to stay with them in an extra bedroom. His wife would do the cooking, but we would have to furnish them with our meat stamps. At this time, just about everything was rationed, so we brought our ration books along. We felt fortunate that Dorothy could move out of the hotel, and that there would be no more bus rides to the camp, as well as no more hotel bills. Good things, of a spiritual nature always seemed to happen, especially when Dorothy was around.

During one of our conversations, Dorothy told me about an incident that had occurred while she was in training. Sister Timothy, who was in charge of the nursing school, came to Dorothy and told her she had to leave and go home. Dorothy told her that she had done nothing wrong. Without any explanation, Sister Timothy told her to go home and stay there until she was called to return. So Dorothy left and told her mother what had happened. Later Dorothy found out that a short nurse with dark hair had crawled through a window at night to get back to her room. Dorothy thought it could have been just any nurse fitting that description, and no explanation was ever given, About one week later, she received a call to return to school.

My eight weeks of training ended, and at about the same time, V-J Day occurred. That meant the end of the fighting war. I received my orders to go to Camp Van Doran in Mississippi where a redeployment center was being established. Then we purchased our train tickets to go back to Chicago.

When I got back to my home in Berwyn, I asked my father if I could use his car again while I was still in the States. This was the same 1939 Buick we had repaired in Indiana during our short honeymoon trip. He was surprised, but I told him he could buy another car for himself. We started on our way to Camp Van Dorn near Centerville, Mississippi.

By this time, it was September, and Dorothy was pregnant with our first child. Right from the start, Dorothy had said that she wanted a large family, being the oldest of seven in a family of five boys and two girls. I am the youngest of three, so I was a bit surprised. However I went along with idea, because Dorothy loved children. Even when she started working, her first job was in the nursery. I felt we would be able to afford a large family because, being a doctor, I anticipated a good income.

At Camp Van Dorn, we were marking time because the redeployment center was cancelled as there was no need to move troops to the Pacific Theatre. It wasn't long before new orders came to transfer to Camp Gordon in Augusta, Georgia. So we packed up the car, which incidentally is still running very well, and off we went to Augusta. We looked for housing and found a cottage that was divided into two apartments, one of which was vacant.

At Camp Gordon, now called Fort Gordon, they established a discharge center to get the men from the European Theatre home for Christmas. All the men had to have physical exams by a doctor before leaving the service. Various stations were set up so that the physicals were divided among the doctors. One MD would take histories, another would do heart and lungs, another would do ear, nose, and throat, etc. My first assignment was to check heart and lungs. Can you imagine listening to hearts for eight hours at a time? The stethoscope would hurt my ear canals by the end of the day. My next assignment was to take histories which was a little easier on my ears. We were able to accomplish our task, and all the men were home before Christmas.

We had our first Christmas together in Georgia. Being from the north, some differences made it interesting. The temperature was above freezing and some of the trees still had leaves. At night, the temperature would occasionally drop below freezing and some puddles would have ice on them. But it didn't last long before it all melted.

Dorothy wanted a Christmas tree, and we went into town looking for one. The only trees they were selling were cedar trees, so we bought one and brought it home. Dorothy said that it did not look like a Christmas tree to her. I told her that at the base there were some southern pines that look more like our trees up north. She said "I want one." I went to Sears and bought a hatchet, feeling it might be faster then a saw. The next weekend, I went to the base and into the woods to check out the trees. I did not know who to ask, so I didn't ask anyone for permission.

These were some pretty big trees, and I thought I could just take the top of a smaller tree that might work. I found a suitable tree, and I chopped it off at shoulder height. Down came the tree top, and now I had a pine Christmas tree. I tied it to the roof of the car and drove home. When I tried taking it into the house, I could not get it through the doorway. The lower branches were too wide, so I had to take off another section from the bottom. I finally got the pine tree into the house and out went the cedar tree into the back yard. Our neighbor asked if she could have it, so I gave it to her. We had the tree, but I still needed a stand. I looked into the corner of the room, and I figured I could wire it to each wall to hold the tree up. That worked all right, but Dorothy said that we also needed some ornaments. We purchased six round ornaments, which was all we could afford. Even still, it was our first Christmas together and we had a Christmas tree decorated with ornaments.

One morning, when I went out to get in my car, I stepped on the running board, and it fell off. The next-door neighbor said not to worry, because he was a welder. He said that at the end of the week, he would take our car to his shop and weld it back on. He was not too reliable, because he was not always sober. But he took the car and did an excellent job of restoring the running board. He also refused to charge us. We thanked him for his kindness, because we had limited funds. But, he did get his Christmas tree from us. Being able to get our car repaired without charge was another event with spiritual overtones.

We had plans to go to midnight mass, and when we went outside, we could hear explosions as if fireworks were going off. We looked up to see sky rockets lighting up the sky over head. This was certainly a surprise, and a strange way to celebrate Christmas Eve.

My assignment at Camp Gordon was winding down, and the rumors were that we would be going overseas. I decided that Dorothy should be going home to Chicago to have our baby which was due in April. She talked to her parents who said that she could stay with them. I decided that the fastest and safest way would be for her to fly back to Chicago. It was still winter, and driving from Augusta to Chicago could present problems. Besides being in the Army, my life was not my own, and I wanted Dorothy to be safe, especially with the baby coming in the spring.

About two weeks after her departure, orders came for me to go to Europe as part of the army that would be occupying Germany after the war. This was a problem. I was still in Georgia with my father's car, and Dorothy was in Hillside with her parents. I decided to get a leave before shipping overseas so I would have time to drive back to Chicago. I planned to drive straight through in one day, assuming I started early in the morning and the car was performing well. It was the end of January, and I was a little concerned about the weather going to Chicago. However I needed to get the car back regardless.

The day I decided to leave the weather was clear, and no storms were in the weather forecast. As planned, I started early in the morning after breakfast, and the car performed perfectly. The roads were dry, and the weather remained clear. I stopped for lunch, and after two or three hours on the road, I saw a hitchhiker up ahead.

Thinking that he would be company to talk to and keep me awake, I decided to pick him up. He was in his twenties and didn't look too shabby. After we started talking, he told me about a hidden knife that he had strapped on his leg. I became concerned, remembering Dorothy's grandfather who had been beaten up by a hitchhiker and was paralyzed for the rest of his life. Then I told the young man that I was a poor GI going home before being shipped overseas. That I had no money, and that my clothes were army uniforms. After a few more miles, he asked to be let out, which I did with a deep sigh of relief as I believed that he was up to no good. Looking back, this whole trip was under spiritual guidance and protection.

The rest of the trip was uneventful. I arrived safe and sound back to Dorothy in Hillside with a few days to spare. Later I returned the car to my father, and thanked him for his generosity. I really appreciated it, and it was a great gift for us. We were able to be together for our first six months of marriage.

My orders came, and I was on my way to the East Coast, to depart from a port in New Jersey. We were going to cross the Atlantic in a large troop transport ship with several hundred GIs and a few officers. The officers were billeted in cabins above deck, with the GIs below deck. The mess halls were separated so we never really saw the GIs except when we pulled guard duty. This required officers to go below deck and watch the GIs. There were plenty of officers so I was assigned only once. While there, everything was peaceful. Some of the men were sitting around and talking. Some played cards while others played various games. The thing that surprised me most after seeing all these men, was how this ship could carry enough fresh food for all of us.

It took us nine days to cross, but there was no rough weather to cause any seasickness. We were able to walk around on the deck at our leisure and enjoy the pleasant weather. The sky was clear, and the ocean was very calm.

When we landed in France, we were told not to leave the controlled areas because the French people hated us. We were the first troops of the occupation of Germany, replacing the troops that were in actual combat earlier. They were leaving as we were arriving. My overseas time would be about fourteen months which would be spent in the American zone in Bavaria.

It was not long afterwards when our first son, Ray Jr., was born on April 16th. I cried when I got the telegram, as I had really wanted to be there with Dorothy. Dorothy's delivery was in Oak Park Hospital where we both were in training. She was very popular, because she was back with many of her classmates. However they kept calling her, "Miss Osborn." She would remind them, "I am Mrs. Broz now." But Dorothy said they would not listen and continued calling her, "Miss Osborn." I received many pictures via mail, and an occasional lock of hair.

At Easter the military personnel were offered a phone service where we could make a phone call on Easter Sunday to our home for 3 minutes for $25.00. I signed up for it. I was able to give Dorothy the approximate time in advance. I was able to talk to Dorothy, but the baby was asleep. She tried to wake him, but he did not make a sound. It was really great to hear her voice, and I was happy to learn that everything was working out well.

The letters went back and forth for the remaining months. Later during my tour, officers could bring their wives and families over and could get a home with one or more servants, depending on rank. I was a Captain then and would have been entitled to have one servant, but babies under one year old were not allowed. My family could come over in April or May of 1947 after Ray Jr. had his first birthday but I would have to remain in the service for another year if Dorothy joined me, with the baby. That was not very appealing to me, so we decided that I'd finish my tour in Bavaria on my own.

I had few medical duties to perform, and I was bored. Besides, I wanted to return to the States to be with my family in the worst way. I didn't want to give the Army another year of my life. The next set of orders that I really wanted was for me to return to the States.

In Germany, everything was in transition, and orders were being changed frequently. I was first stationed in Stuttgart, but a few days later I was transferred to Regensburg. Here I was assigned to the 57th Field Hospital, but that never opened. Then I was assigned to the 1st Medical Battalion of the 1st Infantry Division. I became the Commanding Officer of Company C, also called Charlie Company. This Company was in charge of ambulances. There weren't many opportunities to use the ambulances for medical emergencies, so I asked what were the ambulances used for. I was told that they go to the brewery to bring barrels of beer back for weekend parties.

While I was with Company C, I got an assignment to go to another town and to take an ambulance with about 4 or 5 GIs inside. We were to start immediately which would require some night driving. My sergeant took the first turn at the wheel. After a while, he told me that he was getting sleepy. I told him that I would take over. There I was, driving an ambulance in the dead of winter, at night, with snow-covered roads.

Suddenly, ahead of me was a small deer. Making a quick decision and trying not to skid out of control, I slowed down without braking but I still hit the deer. I stopped the ambulance and woke my sergeant. I told him what happened, and suggested that perhaps we could salvage some venison. He came back and said it was driven over. He said he pulled it to the shoulder and left it for the locals. This was and still is the one and only time I killed a deer.

While in Germany we were issued American script in place of American money. We were not allowed to have any German money, and they were not allowed to have ours. However a system of barter and exchange developed whereby American cigarettes became the medium of exchange. I did not smoke, but each officer was allowed to buy a carton of cigarettes for 35 cents every week. I would buy my allowance and began using these cartons to purchase local merchandise. My GIs knew places to buy things and taught me how to determine prices in cigarettes.

So I traveled to various stores and factories with my cartons of cigarettes. As I used up my supplies, I would write home and ask Dorothy to send me cartons of cigarettes. She knew I didn't smoke and was bewildered at the request. She could not believe it, even after my explanation, but she sent me several cartons. I was able to buy 2 electric miniature trains complete with tracks and transformers, fine tablecloths and lace doilies, all paid for with cigarettes.

These electric train sets fascinated me, and I was anxious to see at least one of them work. I looked around for a large room , and set the tracks around the X-ray table. I had a couple of GIs helping, and we put the engine on the tracks. We plugged it in, and it ran very well. We were all delighted standing around when it was announced that the Colonel had arrived for an inspection of the facilities. He came in, looked all around, and saw the train on the floor. No comments were made, and he proceeded on his way. I never heard any comment about it afterward, either. After all there was not any thing medical going on.

There appeared to be no opportunity for me to have any contact with anything medical. Although I was elevated to a Captain, I was bored being the C.O. of Charlie Company so I asked for a transfer. In January of 1947 I was transferred to the 32nd Field Artillery Battalion where I became Battalion Surgeon located in Munchburg.

This turned out to be my last and best assignment. I had my own Jeep with no restrictions, so I could go where ever I wanted. I would ask the GIs where the good factories were, and how to get there. They told me about a porcelain factory that made beautiful articles. Of course, cartons of cigarettes were necessary. I was able to buy an extremely beautifully-crafted ceramic ballerina doll. It had all these fine delicate features that I really admired. Later when I left for home, I carried it with my clothing so it would not get damaged.

I was told about an excellent china factory, that made beautiful Bavarian china that I could not resist. I was able to buy 2 complete sets, one a serving for six and the other a serving for eight. These were complete dinner sets which included serving bowls. I was able to get nine sturdy wooden ammunition boxes to send all this glassware back home. I had never shipped glass before, so there was some breakage before they arrived home. But, my daughter still uses some of the dishes today, 60 years later.

Munchburg is close to the Czech border, and with all my ancestors coming from Bohemia, I wanted to go to Prague before I left. I was able to get a weekend pass, and with a driver, we took a Jeep into Prague. I was a little disappointed because the locals were all Westernized, they spoke English, and were wearing blue jeans. However I had heard that Czech crystal was very beautiful, so I wanted to bring some home. I found a shop that sold a wine set of a decanter and six stemware—fine hand-cut crystal. Unfortunately, this was purchased with American dollars and it also suffered from my poor packing. Some of the stemware did not make it, but the decanter was fine.

Another time while still at this last assignment in Munchburg, I had an unusual experience. It was on Good Friday that I learned that there were people going to see Therese Neumann of Konnersreuth, which was a neighboring town to Munchburg. I heard about her many years previously, possibly while I was still in grammar school. I remembered that at that time it was said that she had the stigmata of Jesus. Suddenly, I learned that she was still alive, and in the next town.

However, a new order had been enacted, stating that no officer was to be permitted to drive his own vehicle. I checked with our motor sergeant if I could have a driver take me to that town. The motor sergeant said he could take me there that afternoon, and off we went. We were able to find the home by the number of people milling around. This was an ordinary home right in the middle of town. We just walked up the stairs, and we were pleasantly greeted. We were told she was in her bedroom, and we took our place in line. Once inside we were allowed to enter this bedroom. There we saw this lady, lying in bed, with a shawl over her head. Her eyes were closed and there was a blood stained cloth over her right hand.

We were told that she had no food or liquids since 1923. All she received is one Holy Communion Host brought to her daily by the local priest. This continued until she died in 1962. The stigmata began in 1926 with a severe pain in her left chest and eventually a trickling of blood appeared. Then later the stigmata followed the pattern of Jesus' wounds. The fact that I was able to be there and witness this person is a spiritual event for me.

All the medical officers finished their internships at the same time, entered active duty at the same time, and we were all waiting for orders to leave at the same time. We had the option to fly home, but if we did, we would have to stay in Germany for two more months. Otherwise, we could leave by ship right away. Coming over by ship hadn't been too bad, and I would be leaving right away, so I chose this option. There was a last-minute change in our departure port. We had arrived in France but would be leaving from a port in Germany, which didn't bother me at that time. Little did I know...

We boarded the troop ship with the expectation of a nine-day cruise across the Atlantic. But, we had to go through the English

Channel before reaching the open ocean. Our large troop ship rocked and rolled for two days and then on the third day when we finally reached the Atlantic, everyone was seasick. Including me. I ate solid food but none stayed down for those two days. On the third day, I decided to try to eat something. Since the mess hall was serving meals at each meal time, I went to the mess hall and took an apple, went to my bunk, and laid down, I ate the apple slowly. It stayed down. At the next meal, I took an orange and did the same thing. Lo and behold, the orange stayed down. The next day I went to the mess hall and I was able to have a small meal. After about four days without food, I was able to eat regularly. Some officers, including doctors, were taken to sick bay to get IV fluids. The next five days were not bad. Again, I was surprised at all the fresh fruit and vegetables that were being served, especially at the end of the trip.

We had smooth sailing the rest of the way heading for Fort Dix in New Jersey, our discharge center. We had a few days' wait before we were scheduled to go through the discharge system, which is typical of the Army system to hurry up and wait. A fellow Medical Officer that I met aboard the ship invited me go with him. His brother, who worked in Washington D.C., made reservations for him to spend a couple of nights in a pagoda in Washington. He invited me to go along. It was nearby significant places in the Capitol, so we could walk to do some sight seeing.

We headed back to New Jersey to be formally discharged by getting all the papers completed and signed. My obligation to my country had been completed. I was able to get my plane ticket, and I called Dorothy to tell her my time of arrival.

# Chapter 4: Medical Practice

I arrived at O'Hare, and finally walked into the terminal building. When Dorothy saw me she said, "What happened? You are so thin!" What a way to lose weight.

I had finally come home.

It was a pleasure to be home with Dorothy and my son. He was a little over a year old and he had never seen his father. He seemed to wonder who I was, and when I might be leaving. I sensed the resentment, and from his point of view, I was just someone who was taking up so much of his mother's time. Before I returned home, he had her all to himself. But I stayed, and he adjusted.

Once my military obligation was out of the way, we had to begin a new phase in our lives, raising a family. When I was at Loyola U. taking a course in Medical Ethics, I had a very astute Jesuit professor, Father Kelly, who taught us the way to live the rest of our lives. He said that when God created man, He also included a sexual appetite and sexual pleasure. God gave man instructions to multiply and fill the earth. Then Father Kelly added it only seemed logical that since raising children is such a difficult task, God would include some pleasure in the sexual act. The desire to have sex and the pleasure associated with sexual performance is built into human nature. God put it there and therefore it is good. If there were no pleasure, then no one would want to have children. Therefore in God's plan for the procreation of the human race, having children is essential.

When I married Dorothy, who had a similar religious background, we felt that the Church was guiding us with the necessary principles for our lives. A form of birth control had to be part of our lives to demonstrate responsibility for our children. The Catholic Church advocates a system called the rhythm method, which promotes responsibility and self-control. This isn't easy, but it can work. However, it does help if a large family is planned, because errors in the schedule are common. This can lead to unplanned pregnancies.

My good fortune continued. My parents had a two-flat apartment building with a vacant second floor apartment, and they said we could move in. After fourteen months, I was able to live with Dorothy and Ray Jr. in our own home. During the time Dorothy lived with her parents, she was able to save some money. Then, with the help of her uncle Jake, we were able to buy a new Plymouth and pay with cash. We were also able to borrow furniture for the apartment, and Dorothy had a crib and a playpen for the baby. My father surprised us one day by giving us money to buy some rugs, saying that he did not want to keep hearing all those footsteps from upstairs on the bare floors. Our home was only one block from the main street, so shopping was just a short walk. I needed the car every day to go to and from work.

Not having been in practice before I left, I had nothing to return to, I wanted to go into a surgical residency but was advised to go into family practice for a few years. All the surgical residences were filled for about three years. However, after I left Oak Park Hospital, I was appointed to the medical staff, and now I had somewhere to start. I was greeted very warmly by the other staff members. I was given the opportunity to be on call for the emergency room for one month at a time on a rotating basis. This was a valuable service because, if a patient needed to be hospitalized, the doctor on call would be the attending physician. Also, one of the staff doctors found an office for me above a drug store. If a patient needed ambulatory care, I was able to give them follow-up care in my office, and now I had an income which I sorely needed to support my new family.

About a year after I returned from the Army, I was able to purchase an active practice from a doctor who was moving to California. I had no funds of my own, so I had to borrow money from relatives, and with first and second mortgages, we were able to close the deal. The practice I bought included a home and an office. The office was in a separate building that had been a garage but was converted to office space. The garage had to be enlarged to provide additional space. The office was on a corner so there was direct access from a street. Construction was well done, and even included air conditioning. I became the doctor who is practicing in a garage. In a few years I was able to build my own medical center on a main street in town. We kept the old office building and converted it into a 3 room apartment, which included air conditioning.

It was in December that we moved into the new building, and it seemed like the phone never stopped ringing. This was in the era when doctors made house calls. When I was finished in the office and got home, Dorothy would have one or two house calls for me to make. This would keep me going until 10 or 11 o'clock. I was young, and I was enjoying my self. After all I was a doctor, and someone needed me. Later I found out that I was the cheapest doctor in town. My attitude was that I loved taking care of sick people, but, incidentally, I had to charge them for my services. Some people never paid me, and I didn't care. I did not sue anyone for my fee, and I did not get sued in return. Several years into my retirement, I received a check in the mail from a mother who included a note that stated "This is the final payment for my baby. Now he is mine."

It wasn't too much later that we had our second son, and Dorothy was also helping me by cleaning the office. She didn't complain, because I was earning a good income. But we also had a lot of debts that needed to be paid. As my practice grew, so did our family. We had family planning of sorts, and our children were about two years apart until we had twins. After they arrived, the children came three years apart. We had help when the family got larger. In addition, God gave me the most wonderful in-laws in the world. Dorothy's parents, who were good and saintly people, always helped us whenever we asked. They were Dorothy's models, having raised seven children under the very difficult conditions of the Depression and war.

When there were three: Ray, Roger, and baby is Gary.

Our third pregnancy was a little early on our two year plan. By paying closer attention, we discovered that Dorothy had two ovulations every month. This could result in twins which is common in both of our families. In planning our next pregnancy, we found out that was correct, and we had twins, a girl, Barb, and a boy, Bob. When Dorothy and I were discussing the possibility of having twins, she mentioned that there would be additional work in raising two babies at one time instead of just one. So I suggested that I would be willing to give the 2:00 AM feeding so she could get a good night's rest. She said that would help, and she seemed to want to try.

So when the babies came home then the 2:00 AM feedings began. Previously I was able to sleep through one baby crying, but with two babies crying, I was awake. I had to go downstairs to warm the bottles. After about two weeks of this routine, I put my head down on the table one night and fell asleep. When I awoke, the bottles were in a pot of boiling water, so now I had two bottles too hot to handle, I started cooling them off in cold water. Once I felt that the bottles were cool enough, I was able to feed the babies. Eventually, Dorothy got up and asked what was taking so long. Then she looked at Barbara and said, "Her head is all wet and sweaty." I told her that perhaps the milk had been too warm and told her what had happened. Evidently, one bottle had still been too warm. No harm was done and the twins did fine.

Our children when there were 5. Front row (left to right) Bob, Gary, Barb. Back row (left to right) Ray, Roger.

Raising twins is a little different than raising just one baby at a time. It appears that if one of the twins doesn't think of something, the other one will. Once, one of them took a box of Kleenex to the top of the stairs from the second floor and sent all 200 tissues fluttering down the stairway. When they were a bit older, they thought it would be great fun to dump a round can of potato chips on the rug and roll the can back and forth, grinding the chips into the rug.

Dorothy and I believe that they liked the crunching sound of break-ing chips. Despite the trouble, with a little patience, all turned out fine.

Another interesting time was when Barbara came down from the second floor to the landing that faced the kitchen and said, "Mommy look at me." To Dorothy's astonishment, she saw Barbara's arms and her legs all painted black. Then Barbara added, "Gary painted me," as she showed off her arms and her legs. Then a quick trip to the bath tub, and the soap and water took it all off.

Main lodge and dining hall of Drowsy Water Dude Ranch in Granby, Colorado.

Young Dorothy, circa 1950. Beautiful.

Dr. Ray, circa 1950.

# Chapter 5: Our Children

Everything considered we have a wonderful family which is also a family full of wonder. In a large family, each child is a separate individual with their own personalities, and I would like to describe each of our children individually. Actually, Dorothy did most of the raising our children, because my practice kept me very busy with irregular hours.

### *Raymond Jr.*

While I would be driving, I thought I would use the opportunity for him to identify colors. When approaching a traffic signal, I would ask him to identify the color of the light. He seemed to hesitate often, and he was unable to give me an answer. After he started in school, one day I received a letter that had a return address saying something about the prevention of blindness. Dorothy mentioned that his eyes were examined at school, and evidently he had trouble reading the chart. We went to see the ophthalmologist, and he ended up needing glasses with a severe correction to his vision. Later, when he received his glasses, he told me that now he could see the pole at the intersections that had the lights on it. I was asking him to see the colors

The whole Broz clan about 1980 with my parents, Mary and Frank, at our home in Hillside, IL by the swimming pool fence.

Family reunion in the 1990's in Hawthorn Woods, IL at Brozville II.

when he couldn't even see the pole. He needed repeated changes in the lenses as he was getting older; and these special lenses had to be made in California.

Ray went to St. Gregory, a junior College in Oklahoma. Dorothy and I felt it would be fun to take the long route to Oklahoma via New Orleans. Cousin Jack and Betty Jean were already there, so we made plans to visit them. We had never been there, and they would be able to escort us around. We arranged our trip to allow us to have two days there. With Ray in the car, we arrived and met Jack and Betty Jean as planned. We were having a wonderful time seeing the sights, and we would occasionally stop for a drink. They had a special drink called a hurricane served in a special glass, so we had a few of those as we toured. After dinner we continued making the rounds and enjoying ourselves when Jack said that it was about 3am, and perhaps we should have breakfast. He said that he knew just the spot. We were able to have a fine meal, and we got back to our rooms around 4am. We expected to sleep late, when suddenly there was a loud pounding on our door. Then a man's voice telling us that a hurricane was coming, and everyone must be out by noon! I checked the time and it was 8am. We left by 10am, and headed Northwest which was out of the path of the hurricane. We got Ray to school safely, and he was able to be enrolled. He did fine, and in two years he received his Associate Degree. He was now interested in the job market.

I was able to find a help wanted ad that was seeking a person experienced in chemistry to work at Curtis Candy Company. Knowing that Ray had had Chemistry, I suggested he should apply. Well he did, and he got the job. So he became my "candy man".

In his job there was a time that he had to go to the railroad yard, whenever a tank car of corn syrup arrived, to test the concentration of the syrup. This had to be done before the company would accept the delivery. It was necessary for him to climb to the top of the tank car. He would get his sample and then leave.

One time while he was on top of the tank car, it started to move. Here he is in his white lab coat on top of tank car moving right along. He started to holler and scream, while waving his white coat as the train was passing a lookout station. He got their attention, and they were able to stop the train. Now he was able to get off safely, and take his sample back to the company.

While working at the candy company, Ray said he had some vacation time coming. I was always ready for a vacation, and the two of us made a quick 3 day trip to Tampa Florida. While we were on the beach, there were a couple of boys playing in the sand. We struck up a conversation with them, and I told them my son was a candy man, that he made candy. With their eyes wide open they said "Wow."

He was the second of our sons to get married. They had a son, but the marriage was not very stable. Needless to say, the marriage ended in divorce, and their son, Jason, lived with us for about a year. Ray's second marriage was a bit calmer, and they will soon be celebrating their thirty second anniversary. Mostly on his own, Ray found a desire to learn electronics and has become an expert with computers. One company recognized his skill and gave him the title of "Electronic Service Engineer." He has the knowledge and expertise even though he does not have the official degree. He continues to take courses to renew his skills to keep pace with the new developments.

In addition he is a cancer survivor, not once but twice. The first time it was the discovery of a malignant melanoma that was made by his wife, Rita. She noticed a strange looking mole on Ray's back, and she told his doctor about it at the next visit. He looked at it, and he did not think it was serious. She kept her eye on it, and on the next visit, she mentioned it again. This time the doctor got all excited, and he rushed Ray over to the dermatologist. They immediately made an appointment for surgery the next morning. After the laboratory report came back, the surgeon said that another surgery was necessary. This time a very deep excision was performed. There has not been any return of the melanoma in the past 20 years.

In the next case, I was involved as a doctor. I was at his home when Ray complained about a pain in his right lower abdomen. I asked him to lie down for me to exam him. Upon examination I thought he was having acute appendicitis, and he needed to go to the emergency room for more tests. The tests did not confirm appendicitis, and they were about to send him home. However an astute surgeon in charge, advised not to dismiss a man with a pain in the abdomen. He went to surgery that evening, and a tumor was found in the appendix. After the laboratory tests, the tumor proved to be malignant. As a precaution, another surgery was performed, and his right colon was removed in case there was any spread. There was none, and now after about 10 years, he has had no recurrence.

Jason's wedding to Michelle with dad Ray Jr. and wife Rita.

# Roger

Being two years younger than Ray, Roger was given everything similar to what was done for his older brother. His personality is very congenial, and he followed closely in the foot prints of his brother. The attention you would give to one, you would also give to the other.

Our first two sons, Ray and Roger.

About the time that Roger was 4 or 5 years old, we had 2 ponies. Actually I intended to have only one when I saw a ad in the paper saying that there was a carnival pony for sale. I felt that that type of pony would be trained for children to ride. I felt this would be perfect for what I needed. After I located the stable where it was kept, I found out it was a female, and she was in fold. I arranged with my father in law to house the pony, because he had experience with horses years ago. I thought that being in fold would not present a major problem. After all animals have there young in the field, and they can handle this alone. So I bought the pony.

The original pony was all black, and Dorothy named her Queenie. I bought a white saddle, and I knew how to saddle a horse from all those years at the ranch. I put the saddle on Queenie and picked up one of my children. I put him in the saddle, took the reins, and we walked around the yard. I think I was more excited then the children. They appeared a bit frightened by the size of the animal.

When spring arrived, so did the baby pony. Fortunately I was correct, except at the end my father in law had to help in delivering the new born female pony. Every thing ended fine, and mother and baby were in excellent shape. Our baby pony was white with large patches of brown. Dorothy named her Patches. She was pretty, and she was very active. She ran and jumped most of the time. If you came close, she would come at you showing her teeth trying to bite you. Her personality was just the opposite to her mother who would move slowly and was very docile. Patches was acting like the wild animal that she was.

Our ponies just loved watermelon rinds, and Roger, age 5, was bringing a plate full over to Patches. She was tied, but she came quickly. As Roger turned to get away, Patches also turned and kicked Roger with both hind legs right on his butt perfectly placed. Roger turned around and said in a loud voice, " I hate you, I hate you."

These two ponies were more than we could handle, so I made it known that they were for sale. My mother in law had a cousin who had some acreage, and he bought them both for his grandchildren. I was very fortunate, the new owner was able to come and pick up both ponies with all the accessories.

Roger at High School graduation.

Years later when Roger went to college, he attended St. Procopius College and seemed pretty well adjusted. In fact he was very pleased and impressed with his surroundings. After he finished his first year, he went to the Abbot in charge and expressed the desire to become a Benedictine monk. Roger was advised that he would have to obtain the religious records of his parents as well. This would consist of baptismal, conformational, and marriage records. He would also have to write a paper about why he wanted to be a monk.

This all came as a surprise to us, but it was a pleasure to know his intentions. We then proceeded to get all the necessary papers and gave them to Roger. He wrote his paper and everything was ready. Roger took all the material to the Abbot, and as he was handing them to the Abbot he said, "I just changed my mind."

He changed schools, but after one semester, another surprise. He joined the Navy. This was during the Viet Nam war. This is one of the times when the parents are the last to know. He enlisted for 4 years.

His first assignment was to repair and install electrical equipment in Navy airplanes in San Diego, California. It is hard to believe, but he was stationed there for 4 years. During that time he was able to rent a small apartment with another Navy man and they moved off base.

Roger at Mir Mar Naval Air Base. His only duty station for 4 years

Our Navy man, Roger.

We decided to drive out to San Diego to visit, also because we had never been to California. We arrived at his address, and we found the apartment at the rear of a larger home. The door was ajar, and it was tied to a railing. There was a cat in the house. We looked into the refrigerator, and all we found was cans of beer and cat food. In the center of the living room was a short log, like a tree stump. On this stump was a lot of wax from candles with additional candles on the side. I sat on the sofa which was near a window that had some drapes on the sides. While I was sitting there, a cat climbed up the drape and jumped onto the back of my neck with all its claws into my skin. What a shock that was. I leaped up, and the cat ran out the door.

Roger finally got home, and he said that they ate all their meals at the base. Therefore they did not buy any food for the house. They kept the door tied open so the cats could come and go without messing up the house. He then took us on a tour of the harbor, and there were several large ships anchored there. He made the comment that he was in the Navy for almost 4 years, and that he had never slept aboard a ship. He also did very well, and he was promoted to Petty Officer. We received a very nice letter from his commanding officer praising him for his good work.

Roger was ready to be discharged, and he needed to have a discharge physical before leaving. All during his physical he wore his sailor cap even though he had no clothes on. When he reached the final station, and the officer there said "Sailor take off your cap." Roger removed his cap, and his long hair fell over his ears. He was informed that he can not leave the service until he got a haircut. He went to the base barbers, and they said that they would not touch him because he was in violation of Navy regulations. Now he had to go to a civilian barber for a haircut before he can be discharged.

When Roger came home, he informed us not to mention that he was in the Navy because people hated the military. He was depressed and had no inclination to look for employment. Dorothy tolerated this for a few weeks, but then she informed him that her brother, Uncle Pete, had a good job for him when he was ready. In a short time he called Uncle Pete, and he started working on a job.

He found an apartment and started living on his own. A few weeks later my other children were all excited, and they started to leave. We asked " Where are all of you going?" They answered that they were going to help Judith move in with Roger. We answered that they were not married. They added that Roger said that they will get married later. After a few weeks, Roger calls on Wednesday to inform us that they were married on Monday. The marriage has

Roger's family (left to right) Leslie, Karen, David and Margaret.

Roger on right with David and Leslie with Aydan.

lasted over 35 years, and they have 4 children and 4 grandchildren. He was able to finish college by going to school part-time, and he received his degree in Physics.

## Gary

Being Dorothy's third pregnancy, I was expecting a female child, because we already had two male children. I think I convinced Dorothy that we should pick out a name for our girl baby. Still after the delivery, we were overjoyed to have our third son. Now quickly we need a boy's name. I told Dorothy that I just had an emergency where a young boy broke his wrist. She asked, "What was his name?" I answered that his name was Gary. She replied that she liked that name. Three days later our baby boy Broz became Gary Broz.

It seems that set the stage for Gary to be a bit different than our other children. I could call it non-conforming. For example, if our family was ordering strawberry ice cream, Gary would want chocolate.

A major problem started when Gary started his schooling. He seemed to have the ability to annoy teachers by not doing his work, but knowing all the answers. At one time he was sent out of the classroom, and he ended up in the auditorium. He got all dirty by exploring all the props under the stage. Another time one teacher gave an ultimatum to the school. She said that she wanted him out of her class by Christmas, or else she would quit teaching. By the time Gary reached the 8th grade, this teacher-student problem continued, and it became apparent that a change in schools was necessary.

I promptly went to talk to a neighboring parochial school, and I was told they would be happy to take him. The nun in the eighth grade was very enthusiastic, and when he started she gave him extra duties. He became a patrol boy at a busy intersection, and he was in charge of a pencil machine. He became her star pupil. His final report card was full of A's.

He did well in high school except for getting hurt playing football. The first year he had a fractured wrist. The next year he had a badly fractured ankle which had to be surgically reduced and about 6 weeks on crutches. He was able to attend school even including going up and down stairs on crutches. I told him that football was a bad idea.

He enrolled in college and attended one semester. One night I was awakened at 4:00 am with horns tooting in front of our home. I investigated only to find out that this was a ride for Gary to leave to take his physical exam for the Navy. He served in the Navy for 8 years during the Viet Nam war.

He would write home to tell us that he was on a Frigate that was shelling the shore. Later he would write that his ship was in Subic Bay in the Philippines for repairs. When he returned home after his discharge, he explained that the trips to Subic Bay was for repairs because the ship was hit by shells from the shore. Some times the engines would get damaged, and they would limp along to get repairs. He said that in his letters he did not give any details, because he didn't want us to worry about him. He returned home safe and sound.

He was married while in the service, and that marriage is past 38 years. They have 2 children and 4 grandchildren. After he raised his children, he entered college again. This time he graduated as an Electrical Engineer.

While he was in the Navy, he developed a smoking habit, because he said they always had a 10 minute break for a cigarette. This habit has continued ever since he left the Navy. Recently he needed to have heart surgery, a quadruple bypass, due to an early heart attack. He is the first to have heart surgery in our family.


## Barbara

Our Barbara was the first of the twins to be born, and I was pleased because now I had a daughter. Then about 5 minutes later the other twin was born, and then we had our Robert. They would end up being our Barb and Bob. Previously I mention our earlier experiences with raising twins, but they each had their own personalities.

Barb tended to be more protective of her brother as they grew older. When they started to go to school, I asked if it would be possible for them to be in different rooms. This was able to be accomplished.

Barb was also musically inclined, and she learned to sing and later to play the guitar as well. She had singing lessons in high school, and she performed in a musical where she sang a solo. Even today she has a beautiful voice, and I enjoy being with her in church. She has memorized most of the church hymns, and she is also good at sight reading.

As we were going on vacations to dude ranches in Colorado, Barb asked if she could work there during the summer break from college. The owner said that they do hire college girls as cabin girls, but they also perform as entertainment after dinner in the evening. It was usually music with singing. That was the incentive, and she learned to play the guitar.

She was hired the next summer and enjoyed her work, because one day each week they were treated as guests. They were able to ride the horses and go on the mountain trails. There was also an above ground swimming pool for relaxing. When our family arrived, there were various tricks being played on each other. One was about short sheeting the beds. That is when the bottom sheet is folded in half and does not go to the foot of the bed. Another was making fake spider webs with spiders on them over the top bunk.

She entered college, and she was an excellent student. After her second year, she was awarded an academic scholarship. This covered all her tuition, and now her room and board were the only expenses. However Barbara fell in love during her sophomore year with a senior, and he proposed to her. She told us that she wanted to get married. I mentioned that this was giving up a very good thing considering she only had 2 years of college, and now she had a scholarship. As children do, she said that marriage was what she wanted to do, and a church wedding took place.

In a short time Barb was pregnant, but a caesarean delivery was necessary. She eventually had 5 children, all caesarean births. All her children grew to be wonderful people. Unfortunately the marriage changed, and a divorce was necessary.

Later Barb found another fine gentleman, and she was able to get the first marriage annulled. Another church wedding took place. At first things were working fine, or so it appeared, but again problems developed. Now a second divorce is necessary.

With Barb in the work force, she found out that 2 years of college is not adequate for a well paying job. She took an aptitude test, and it showed that she would be good as a social worker. She felt that this was accurate, so she went back to college to get that last 2 years by going week ends. She accomplished the work, graduated with her degree, and is a superb social worker. She likes the people and they like her. Besides the pay is better. In addition to her 5 children, at present, she has 7 grandchildren.

Granddaughter Sara's wedding with brother Chuck.

Wedding picture of Barbara and Duane Heirer. This is Barb's second marriage.

Four generations of oldest daughters Morgan, Barbara, Great Grandma Dorothy and Sara.

## Robert

Bob was born after Barb, and he became our fourth son. With the arrival of the twins, the work load really increased, but a surprising thing happened. The residential dish washer became available, and it was marvelous for sterilizing baby bottles. I believe I bought the first one that arrived locally. Another great help was the use of a diaper service which came every day to deliver clean cloth diapers and pick up the dirty ones. We had a bag full every day, because we had three children in diapers at this time.

We very fortunate when one of our neighbor ladies came to visit and asked if we could use some help. She was hired, and she worked for us for over ten years. As Bob was growing up, he had all this personal attention, and he did not need to ask for much help. This timid nature of his became apparent in the third grade when his teacher admitted that she really did not know him until Christmas break. During that time, he fell behind with his the class work. He needed to go to summer school that year, and he was able to pass to the next grade. This little incident changed Bob from then on, and he became more responsible. He did fine after that and became more independent.

At the time before entering high school, he expressed the desire to become a religious brother, not necessarily a priest. Somehow he was directed to St. Henry's Seminary in Bellville, Illinois. This was near St. Louis, and it was run by the Oblate Fathers.

He was doing fine in all the same classes with all the students that were headed for the priesthood. They had extra courses beyond the regular work for this level in school. His grades were good, and he was now in his Junior year. In March of that year with 2 months to finish the school year, we got an urgent letter to come and pick him up. He wrote that he wanted to get out of that school immediately.

I was in Ft. Lauderdale at that time taking a Continuing Medical Education Course. This is an annual requirement for renewal of all medical licensing. I was shocked and disappointed, and I asked him if there was any way possible for him to finish his Junior year there. He accepted that thought, and he did get all his credits for the year. For his Senior year, he was enrolled in the parochial high school where my other children went. All his credits were transferred, and he needed only a couple of courses to graduate.

After graduation he said definitely he did not want to go to college. He found the job market was meager, and all summer he had no prospects. Earlier I had suggested printing as an option, and I repeated it again. Printers have been in our family for two generations. This time he went to the Chicago Tribune where my uncle was still working. He was greeted with open arms, and he started his apprenticeship. He started in a composing room where my father worked, and my uncle Bill was still working the night shift. He continued in that field ever since. Now with computers, many changes and closures have occurred, however he just moved with the flow. He moved from shop to shop and kept up with the changes.

Bob is married to Krissy for over 38 years, and they have 2 children and 1 grandson.

# Richard

It was about 3 years after the twins when we were ready for our 6th child, and our Richard was born. We are now having a busy home, but Dorothy is happy with her plan for 8 children.

He was a very good baby, and he did not need any special attention. Later during his school years he was not a good student, and although he was not a behavior problem, he rarely did any homework, and practically never studied. His grades were average, at best, probably due to his chronic low interest in studying.

He did have a small mishap while we were on vacation at the dude ranch in Colorado. On this one day, he was riding a horse named, Rita. Rita had a practice of inhaling deeply when the wrangler would cinch the saddle. Most times the wrangler would time the final tightening pull on the cinch to coincide when she was between breaths. On this day the wrangler forgot this step, and tightened the cinch during her inhale. This resulted in a cinch which was loose, which Rita seemed to prefer. During the following trail ride, there were no problems while riding in the line going up the mountainside. But when we got to the meadow, and we could run the horses when it happened.

When Rita got to a canter, the saddle started to slip down her right side. Rick had to jump from the running horse, and fell on his shoulder and tumbled, head over heels. I was riding at the end of the line, and I saw the whole affair. By the time I could get to him, he was able to get up on his feet, and he was regaining his breath. He said he was alright and was just a little dusty. The wrangler caught Rita, re-tightened the cinch this time on the exhale, and we continued with the remainder of the ride back down the mountain. Rick made it back to the corral without further adventures.

While in 6th grade, the parochial school started a band program, and the band director was named John Pape. Rick wanted to join the band, and I suggested he try the baritone horn. When I was in the high school band, I liked the baritone horn. So I purchased a baritone for him, and he did great.

He loved music, and in high school he went on to play baritone, trombone, guitar, bass guitar, and bass violin. He was part of the concert band, dance band, and orchestra for his school, and also played in the Elmhurst College concert band and college marching band, the Broadview community orchestra, and for a while performed in a Dixieland Jazz band with some friends. While a senior in High school, he was awarded the Band Leadership award, and he also took first place at the annual Talent Show. Rick, to this day says that the only reason he went to high school was to play in the band. And of course, for all of those after school practice sessions, Dorothy played chauffer and truck driver when it came to delivering him with all his instruments. Behind every great man, a great Mom!

When it came to liturgical music, he participated in the parish folk liturgy every Sunday for about 6 years. He was one of the musicians in the group and also teamed up with several singers to play at weddings. After college he teamed up and formed a group with a lifelong friend, Phil, and they called themselves "Mother and Child." They performed at local venues, bars and sang a number of Irish inspired folk songs, complete with comical bits.

College time was decision time. So far none of my children were planning to go into the medical field. I talked to Rick about being an ophthalmologist, because he said that he didn't like anything too bloody. He began in Bio-PreMed at Loyola University and lasted there for 2 years. He explained that the PreMed program was rife with intense competition, where all means of sabotage, cheating, theft of exams, etc… were the standard operating procedures of the student body. An example of this stuff, would be to un-focus the microscope after viewing, to make it harder for subsequent students to view the microscopic slide during the timed lab exams, or to bump the slide to change the structure indicated for identification. This was all a big surprise to me. Rick still was not the studious type and decided on his own that he was not motivated to do the quantity and quality of study that would permit him to get into Medical School.

Rick transferred to University of Illinois for his junior year, and graduated with a BS in Biology. While in college at U of I, he married Hedy, and they have 6 children. They are about to celebrate their 35th wedding anniversary. They also have 6 grandsons, 1 granddaughter and another baby on the way.

I like to sing. Here at Paul's wedding, I sang "Let Me Call You Sweetheart".
Granddaughter Ann is in the background.

Grandson Frank, wife Cathy and Great Grandson Jeremiah. Cathy took the sunset photo on day of Dorothy's death.

## John

The Lord blessed me with 6 sons. My father made a comment while I was growing up, that I was one of two boys that would carry on the name of "Broz". All of my cousins were girls. I know that my father is pleased that our name "Broz" will be carried on for many years to come. I have 24 grandchildren, 12 of these are grandsons.

As our family grew, there was a lot of interest and help with the arrival of a new baby. Its becoming like many hands make light work. There was very little problem getting our John, nickname Jack, through his infancy into childhood. His learning ability was fantastic, and it would prove that he had good intelligence.

It was in 4th grade that he came to me, and said that his teacher wanted to talk to me. One day after school hours, I went to meet his teacher. She complained to me that Jack was sitting at his desk with an open Geography book over his head. She wanted me to know about this strange behavior. Actually I think she just wanted to meet me. Being "on-call" every day, I asked Dorothy to go to all the parent-teacher conferences. After we left the school, I asked Jack, " Why did you have the book on your head?" He replied that the girl behind him was hitting him on the head with her ruler. He didn't snitch on her.

As he got older, he developed a fascination for manhole covers. These are the large covers in the street all over the city. One day the police called Dorothy that her son, John, was there at the police station, and they wanted her to take him home. She went there to get him and to find out what happened. The policeman said that he and another boy were removing the manhole covers in the street. Many years later, while Jack was in college, he moved from the dorm and rented an apartment with 3 other students. When we visited, there was a coffee table in the living room, and the top of the table was a manhole cover.

He also was an excellent student, and he was on the Dean's list before he graduated as a Civil Engineer. He also has accomplished several projects that required expert skill, and his reputation is widespread. One of these projects was in his own city where he lives, Eden Prairie, Minnesota. For over 60 years, there was a gap in a highway over rugged terrain. This was about 5 miles long and the 4 lane highway ended and 5 miles later it began again. My son was the chief engineer and was successful in completing that highway. The town had a celebration on the opening of the new link that was considered impossible to do.

Jack has always had a strong interest in our lake property, Brozville, which we owned for over 30 years. I could not continue to afford to live there, so I asked Jack to take it over. He accepted and has been able to afford all the costs and maintenance needed. He also has changed the use from a year round home back to a 3 season facility. He has invested a lot of time and money to upgrade and add new amenities. He has restored Brozville as a vacation area for the family for possibly another 30 years.

Jack and his wife, Marilou have been married almost 30 years, and they have three children and one granddaughter.

## Susan

Our eighth child was a girl. That alone was a pleasant surprise. She was our baby and I called her "Babe." For 5 years I called her Babe until she entered the school system. After the first day in school, she was very excited, and she came running to tell me that now she had a name, "Susan."

Now we had 10 for dinner every night unless one of our children wanted a friend or two to stay. Then we had 11 or 12 for dinner. However I worked very irregular hours so during the week I would often eat dinner alone. But on weekends, we would be together, and Dorothy would put out great meals.

Our summer vacations continued by going to a Colorado dude ranch called "Drowsy Water Ranch." They labeled our cabin with a branding symbol, the Rocking B. The B had a rocker under it. They said that with all the trips that we made, we practically paid for the cottage. We would fly to and from Denver. Then we would rent a station wagon in Denver to use to get to the ranch and use while we were there. The air line usually gave us a courtesy by boarding us first, One year on our flight home, we had a skull of a horse's head as part of our hand luggage to carry on the plane.

Sue was about 4 when she started riding horseback. Her little legs were too short to reach the stirrups, so they went straight out from the saddle. The ranch had some very gentle horses for her to ride. She fell in love with horses, and several years later as she got older, she found a stable in a neighboring town that she would visit. She would help out with the chores and exercise the horses.

As she progressed through the school system, it appeared that she could not decide on a career. She was not interested in going to college because she did not find any course to follow. Eventually she started in an art school, but soon she dropped out because the other students were more advanced.

Our Susan as a Bride's Maid.

She located a franchise called "Mail Boxes, Etc." that she felt all enthused about. Now being retired and not having any set obligations, I thought we would try it. There had to be two people involved, so I and Sue went to San Diego for training. We opened a store in Oak Park, Illinois, but it never became profitable.

During the time she was running the store, she developed a medical problem. Periodically she would develop severe pain in her abdomen. This would develop suddenly, and by the time she was able to get to the emergency room, the pain would be relieved. This kept returning several times with no diagnosis. One of these episodes occurred while she was visiting us in Wisconsin. Now I am being a doctor again. On examination of her abdomen, she was having a typical gall bladder attack. Once the gall stone would pass, the pain would be gone. She needed surgery later.

While she was running the store, she did meet a gentleman who began to court her and proposed. Sue accepted and eventually married him. Her love of horses showed up again. She arranged for a horse and carriage to take her from her home to the church. She was in a beautiful bridal gown, and she made a beautiful bride. Her husband is an Aeronautical Engineer with a college degree.

Our Sue in a gorgeous wedding gown and Scott at their wedding.

Eventually he was employed by Lockheed in Denver, Colorado. They were able to buy acreage just East of Denver with a beautiful view of the Rocky Mountains to the West. The acreage was actually a 40 acre parcel of a larger 350 acre wheat farm. On the north west corner of their parcel, they put their home, and their living room has windows facing both East and West. They can view an early sunrise or a sunset over the mountains. Being on the leeward side of the mountains, the rainfall is diminished, and there are very few trees. However there are forests all over the mountains which are near, and in the fall they are able to get to see the color changes.

Later Sue's husband, Scott, developed medical problems, and their marriage developed problems as well. After a one year separation, a divorce ended the marriage of 17 years. Their lives were very upset, but it appears that everything is settling down now after the divorce. They have one son.

Sue, Scott, and son Spencer Havener at a happy time.

Daughter Sue, Grandpa, husband Scott with their 3 legged cat and grandson Spencer.

# Chapter 6: CFM

Early in our marriage, we were members of CFM, Christian Family Movement, when it was in its formative stages. This started as a lay organization which was accepted as a legitimate Catholic movement. The headquarters was in Chicago, and it spread from there nationally, eventually becoming international. It was intended to be primarily for families, but others could join as well. The format of the group was to have no more than five couples per group. Meetings were held in individual couples' homes, and the meetings were scheduled loosely about every two weeks. Every couple received a yellow book which became a standard for all groups. There was a Gospel reading at each meeting, and hopefully, a priest would attend each meeting to prevent any errors in interpretations. Membership in CFM grew to several hundred throughout the country.

It was in the early 1960's when I moved my office, and I finished remodeling the old office into an apartment. This was also the time when many Cuban people were fleeing Cuba because Fidel Castro was taking control over the whole country. We were very active in CFM at that time, and word got to us that there was a great need for housing these immigrants. A group of Cubans had arrived in Chicago, and in that group was a Cuban doctor who was in need of housing. I sent out word, through the CFM communication channels, that I had a vacant apartment for him.

Now these folks were not permitted by Cuban authorities to take anything with them, only the clothes on their back. They even confiscated their wrist watches and other jewelry. I made it known that the apartment was completely empty, except for a stove and refrigerator. As good Christian people tend to give support to those in need, within 24 hours we received donations of furniture, pots and pans, dishes, and even a TV set. Dr. Yaniz and his wife, America, were able to move into a completely furnished apartment.

Dr. Yaniz was fluent in English, but he was an older gentleman close to retirement age. I learned that he was a pathologist in Cuba and owned three laboratories. In my new offices, I had designed space for a medical laboratory, but I only hired a temporary medical technician. Her name was Mary and she was a friend (also a patient) doing me a favor. She was happy to hear Dr. Yaniz was going to be the regular lab technician. Dr. Yaniz was a licensed M.D. in Cuba, but not in the States. I felt that he would be able to qualify as a technician, because we did only relatively simple diagnostic tests. Not only would he have a job with a pay check, he and his wife had a place to live, rent free.

Later in the summer, their two small grandsons came to live with them. Their daughter's family had moved to Venezuela, but she wanted her sons to live in the States for safety reasons. I am not sure why the parents were unable to get passage, but the two boys, Aldo and Juan, were able to come. It appeared that they could only speak Spanish when they arrived. They were in the 4th and 2nd grades, but they were able to be enrolled in our local school. Not only were they able to learn the language quickly, they kept up with their studies, and passed to the next grade. It was delightful to see the boys walking and kicking the leaves in the fall. Also, after the first snow fall, it was interesting to see them trying to make a snow ball. Both events were first experiences for them, having come from a tropical island. However, their poor grandmother, America, was never able to learn to speak English, even after taking a course at the high school.

The next summer Dr. Yaniz decided to retire and move to Florida to be with his friends in the little Cuba part of Miami. In those years, we made frequent trips to our condo in Fort Lauderdale, so we arranged to have them to visit us while we were there. Later we got together in Florida where they invited us to a gala dinner in a fabulous Miami restaurant. The meal was excellent, including the wandering mariachi musicians.

In 1964, CFM organized a trip to Rome while the Second Vatican Council was in session, and we joined that group. They chartered an Air France plane to go from New York to Rome, nonstop.

We all had to go to New York on our own to get to Kennedy Airport for departure. Our Chicago group decided that we were large enough to hire a bus. Our bus was to get us to New York the day before our flight. Our schedule was to ride all night, and we would have one night in a hotel. Another couple from our group, Paul and Helen, made reservations for all four of us to stay at the Waldorf Astoria Hotel, because neither one of us had ever been to New York before.

We boarded our bus in Chicago, and we started our trip to Rome. About 3am we were informed that we had to get off the bus for some unknown reason. In about one hour, we were able to return to the bus and try to get additional sleep. We finally arrived in New York, and the bus took us directly to our hotel. Our companions, Paul and Helen, continued to be a great help in making arrangements for us. It gave us a thrill to be able to stay at the Waldorf—That's real class.

Our charter plane, Air France, was to fly non-stop from New York to Rome, also an overnight trip. There were pictures being taken, and the boarding went smoothly. Up, up and away. We were headed for Rome, we thought. Again at 3am, it was announced that we were landing in Paris at Orley Field. As we approached the air port, I looked out the window, and was I surprised. All the lights were on, and along the margin of the runway, there was a line of fire trucks and ambulances with lights flashing. What a scary greeting. We landed OK, and we deplaned. It was after we were all in the terminal building that we were told that our plane had a tire blow out as we were taking off in New York. They had to replace the wheel before we could continue. Perhaps it was good that we were in France while we were flying Air France. They had the proper parts for replacement. After about a 2 hour delay, we were back on our way to Rome.

In Rome we were paired with our guides who said that because of the delay, there was no time to go to our hotels. At that point, we were scheduled to tour St. Stephan's Catacombs. So, carrying our baggage, without breakfast, we all crammed into a bus going to the catacombs. We had Mass in the catacombs, and then loaded back onto the bus. We should have been headed for our hotel rooms, instead we got into a traffic jam. Cars were standing everywhere. We stood in front of the Spanish Steps, unable to move, and watched the changing of the guards several times. Finally the jam opened up, and we were able to move. The rumor, true or not, was that someone committed suicide by jumping off of a bridge. We finally got to our hotel about 2pm. This building must have been an older style, because the bathrooms were down the hall. It might have been used as a dormitory earlier.

We were in Rome for 2 days of sightseeing on our own. I was happy our other couple, Paul and Helen, did some research before we got here, because they were able to lead us around as our guide. On the morning of the second day, we were alone in St. Peter's Square just standing and looking around. We saw busloads of Cardinals arriving for the Vatican Council. They were all wearing their brilliant red robes, and they were in groups of 20 or more. They made a beautiful picture, because normally you see one Cardinal alone.

While we were standing there among about 100 other people, a priest came up to us and said, "Hello Dorothy." I was shocked and amazed. Then Dorothy said, "Hi Father." The priest continued, "Would you like to go inside?" Dorothy, with a big smile on her face said, "Yes, we would."

He then lead us through a corridor to Saint Peter's Church into a hall. We had to pass several Swiss guards on our way. When we reached a door way, he opened it for us, and he motioned for us to go in. We were inside the Church where all the Cardinals were, and the Pope was saying Mass! We sat in a special section for laypeople on left side of the altar with about nine or ten others. The Cardinals were to our right, seated on what appeared to be bleachers, and there must have been over a thousand present. What a great privilege and honor for us to be there. We were the only people from our entire CFM group in church attending Mass with the cardinals that were there for the Second Vatican Council.

After we left the church, Dorothy explained that the priest we met was actually Monsignor Quinch, a Servite priest, who had known Dorothy's family for many years. He had been working in Africa and had the role of a Bishop. It was our impression that he was present to participate in the council as well.

I cannot help but believe that this happening would not be a spiritual event of the highest degree. This was not just a coincidental meeting.

Later we rejoined our group, and we were able to do the planned sight seeing around Rome. This included a private audience with Pope Paul VI in the Sistine Chapel. We were given special instructions to stay as a group because the Pope would get frightened. Also, we were not to try to touch the Pope. He came in and greeted us in English. He walked up to the front row and spoke to several of our group. Then he turned around and a picture of our whole group was taken with the Pope in the center. I have these pictures framed in my room. After several years, looking back, I told Dorothy this trip was the highlight of our lives.

Eventually we stopped at a restaurant to have dinner. There were six of us, but none of us could speak or understand Italian. We thought it would be appropriate to have spaghetti and meat balls in Rome. After many hand signals, we got a meal, but not spaghetti. When we were almost finished eating, out came a giant bowl of spaghetti. Arriving as we were leaving was another group of CFM members, so we told them to have our meal of spaghetti that we had ordered because it was still on our table.

We continued our trip by taking the train to Lyon, France. We were met by people holding up signs with our last names. This was the beginning of our People to People trip where we stayed at individual homes for visiting and lodging. We were met by a young couple who spoke very little English, and we spoke very little French. So using our translation dictionaries we were able to manage. It was an interesting dinner where we stopped eating to translate what was being said. Before we left, we invited them to come to visit us in our US of A, the way they said it.

From there we went by bus through France, Belgium, and then London. Most of the people we met spoke English, and the families were pleasant and accommodating. We invited each family who hosted us to visit us at our home in return. Eventually, two families from France and a third from Belgium came to stay with us.

One of the French families was large like ours, and the father was a pharmacist. One day, one of his sons called me from the Greyhound Bus station in Chicago, unexpected. I went there to pick him up with his two buddies. They stayed about one week until we told them we were going on vacation. To my surprise, they said we should take them along. I told them that was impossible. They were touring the US by bus, so I told them would have to be on their way.

We continued our bus tour through France to Belgium and we took the train to London. The last home in London was a little different. The family recently moved from India, and the food was unusual. On the table for breakfast was a dish of something red. I tried a little and found out it was raw beef. For breakfast?

After two hectic weeks in Europe, our whole group was able to gather together at the airport. Then we flew to New York from London. Overall it was a wonderful and extraordinary trip with events which were beyond our expectation. I really believe our heavenly Father played a part in the experiences that we had. We have pictures of our trip that are framed to be able to preserve our memories and show to our progeny. I am very thankful that we were able to make this trip.

# Chapter 7: Wisconsin

Vacations and trips are very important in my life. While I was in medical school, our professor told us that when you get sick and tired of hearing people complaining, then that is time for your vacation no matter what your age. I was in solo practice all the while, which meant my on call hours were 24/7, year round, including all holidays.

Continuing along that line, summer vacations became important as our children were growing up. I tried to make it a change of pace for all of us. In 1951, we were on vacation at a lodge in Heafford Junction, Wisconsin. This was an American plan which meant they served all meals as well. We returned every year because we enjoyed their accommodations. Then one year, we had planned a fourteen-day stay at the lodge, and it rained ten days during that time.

Dorothy mentioned that her aunt Pearl and uncle Jake owned a lakefront cottage close to where we were staying. On one of those rainy days, we set out to find it. She remembered the way, and we arrived unannounced, which didn't matter since there was no one around. It was still raining lightly, however my three sons and I decided to explore the area. We were able to find several buildings, and down the hill there was a lake. We found a sheltered place, and Dorothy was able to take some pictures. I don't think any of us really knew it at the time, but that cottage was going to play a major role in the rest of our lives.

July 4th about 1985 in Lac du Flambeau after the parade.

   In the summer of 1971 aunt Pearl called, and she said that since uncle Jake died, she had difficulty in taking care of the lake cottage. She said that she wanted to sell it. I told Dorothy that we should buy it. All I knew about the property was that it was on a lake, and that I had seen it twenty years earlier. I had a secret desire since my childhood, that some day I would like to own a boat, and here was an opportunity that could make it possible. It did not matter much what the condition of the buildings were, because these can be repaired. I called aunt Pearl back, and I asked her to have an appraisal made. I told her that I would pay that amount. She called us later, and told us that the appraisal cane in at $18,000.00. I told her that if that was all right with her, I would pay that amount.

That Fall, we drove back to the lake cottage in Lac du Flambeau to meet with Dorothy's aunt Pearl. We went to her attorney's office and gave her a check in payment for the property. In return we received the title papers which included a history of the property.

This started in 1908 with aunt Pearl's parents, Mr. and Mrs. Thompson, who were white, purchased this Reservation property from a member of the native American tribe named Frank Cross. This initial sale had to be approved by the President of the United States. They bought it as empty lakefront property and built the first cottage. They owned it for thirty tears. During that time their daughter Pearl then married Jake Smith, who became Dorothy's uncle. Uncle Jake and aunt Pearl owned it also for about thirty years. So in the Fall of 1971, we became the owners of beautiful acreage on Big Crawling Stone Lake, later to be called Brozville.

When the Thompson's owned this property in 1908, they built the first cottage on the lake shore. That cottage, although remodeled and repaired, is still on the original site. Over the years, there were

In Wisconsin Brozville early spring clean up.

various buildings added which include a guest cottage, a wet boat house, and a summer kitchen.

Upon examining the deed further, it showed that the property dimensions are 100' wide by 1000' long. It goes East to West and it is close to two acres. On the West it begins at the shore of Crawling Stone lake, and goes east toward an unnamed pond. I like to call it Broz Lake, because the East boundary of the lot appears to extend into the water. Our road, called Indian Waters Lane, bisects the property, and on the East half is a mix of forest and wet lands. All the buildings are on the west half, closer to Crawling Stone Lake.

The Smiths were very religious people who developed various religious artifacts all around. There were many pictures, crucifixes, and statues in different places, but the main one was a small grotto to the Blessed Virgin. This was on the lakeshore in front of the main cottage among the trees on the left. It consisted of a small wooden shelter with an open front and a platform on the bottom. The roof was pitched made of wooden shingles, and all of this was on a mound surrounded with large native rocks. It was large enough to place a two foot tall statue of the Blessed Virgin on the platform. The whole grotto was about four feet tall. The statue was a little weather beaten so Dorothy painted it white. It was movable, and it was brought inside the boat house during the winter.

The Smiths had a son, also named Jake, who became a priest and was a member of the priests at Notre Dame University in South Bend, Indiana. Aunt Pearl spoke frequently how wonderful it was when her son brought his fellow seminarians to the lake shore in front of the grotto. They would build a bonfire at sunset, and they would pray and sing hymns. Father Jake was a retreat master in charge of giving retreats for lay people. One of my colleagues attended several of his retreats and said that Father Jake was a wonderful preacher. I was impressed with this little grotto and kept repairing and rebuilding it as the years went by.

During one of the winter breaks, Dorothy, I, and another couple decided to take a Caribbean Cruise in January. We were booked on a flight that was due to arrive in Miami two hours before departure, which I thought was enough time to get from the airport to the dock.

Our flight was on time until we got over Orlando when the captain announced that there were severe thunderstorms over Miami, and that we would be circling over Orlando for a while. We asked the flight attendant if they could call the dock to have them wait for us. She thought that they could do that for us. She came back with a message that we should call them when we were in the terminal.

When we finally landed in Miami, we called the dock and they said the ship had just left. However the owner of the cruise line was there and wanted to talk to us. We told him that there were four in our party and had two cabins reserved. He said to stay where we were, and that he would pay for all expenses in Miami. Then the next day, we would be picked up and flown to Kingston, Jamaica. Then we would be driven by limousine to Port Antonio, the first stop for the ship. After an over night stay in the hotel there, we would be able to board the ship.

Everyone thought we were special friends of the president, and we got the royal treatment from that point on. The hotel in Port Antonio had a red carpet leading to the entrance, and all our baggage was being carried. Then the next day, we were escorted to the ship and again our luggage was carried all the way to our cabins. At dinner that night, there was a large bouquet of gladiolas in the middle of our table. We were the only people with flowers on the table. At the end of the cruise, a formal dinner was scheduled, and we were asked to join the captain at his table. We had a very enjoyable trip with the temperature in the 80's. Then back to Chicago where the temperature was near zero. What a shock!

Our children had become more independent and Dorothy's interests turned to other children in need. In the summer, Chicago started programs for children, of which Head Start was one, in the inner city and primarily for African-American children. She volunteered to become a leader of a group. The following year, she volunteered again and took our son, Roger, along as her helper. That summer, at the end of the program, the children did not want them to leave. They climbed up on the hood of the car, and kept calling my son 'Daddy.'

Dorothy made banners for our church. Each piece sewn by hand and took hours of work.

Going back to when we first assumed ownership of our lake cottage, it was used only in the summer. Locals call it a three-season cottage because it isn't used in the winter. Even though major repairs were needed, Dorothy planned to go there right after the summer vacation started. I was still working, not being old enough to retire, but Dorothy went there with the two youngest children. While she was trying to keep everything working, she was also interested in the local church, St. Anthony in Lac du Flambeau. She discovered that there was a Sunday school for the Native American children for grades 1-6, so when they asked for teachers, she signed up to teach the fifth grade.

Now during the winter in Chicago, Dorothy learned of a Catholic program which was called SPRED. This was for the religious training of mentally-challenged children. She had to attend special classes to learn the necessary methods they used. As she worked in the program, she developed her own techniques. She also was recognized by others and became a peer advisor.

Sunset at Brozville.

The program consisted of weekly meetings in the local parish for these children who needed a special room with special conditions. Among them was a quiet place as any loud noise is disruptive to these children. She had soft music from a tape player, and a bible opened on a table, along with a lit candle. Then she would softly read to them, and later explaining what she was reading. If anyone became noisy, she would stop talking and silently fold her arms across her chest. As things quieted down, she would then continue.

Once a year, they would have a mass for all these children from the various parishes in the city and the suburbs. Here the more able children would also participate by bringing the altar clothes to the altar, and then later proceed to the altar with the priest, all in silence. At the time of the homily, the priest would say a brief and easily understood homily. When I attended, it was, "God loves you." He repeated it three times, once to the right, then to the center, and finally to the left, pointing to the children as he spoke. Then, moving slowly, he would return to his chair at the altar. To attend a mass of this nature is indeed a privilege. The church recognizes some of these children as possible saints because of their limited mental ability to distinguish between good from evil. When I was leaving the church with Dorothy, I felt I had an ethereal experience.

Every fall, Dorothy would return to her SPRED program in the city. She had her own group of children she taught on Wednesdays, but the rest of the week she would visit various parishes that had no program. She would go to the pastor and ask if they had a program for mentally-challenged children. The usual answer was that they didn't need one because he didn't think there were any. She would assure him that he would be surprised and said she would like him to check with the parishioners. Then she said that she would be back. Upon returning, the pastor was surprised and told her that indeed there were some such children. Then she would follow with the offer to start a SPRED program there. With her training as peer advisor, she usually would train the mother of a student to take over the group after a group was started.

In 1981, I retired and I was able to start my new life living in Wisconsin. Things were not perfect, but I was able to keep up with repairs as they were needed. We had a very friendly and outgoing pastor, Father John, and we invited him over for dinner. After the meal, we sat around and chatted. Being new in the parish, he inquired about our background. We told him of all of our activities, especially Dorothy's, and he told her, "You are a saint." Dorothy brushed it off as if it were of no significance and continued with her regular activities year in and year out.

After a few summers, I thought we could try living in the cottage all winter. What a surprise that was. Our first winter was full of new experiences with dealing with the snow and sub-zero temperatures. We purchased an electric blanket for our bed, but during the day, our feet never got warm. We had a furnace that was oil fired, and we had to wipe the soot off the table in the morning before we could serve breakfast. I also learned that frequently there is about 2 or 3 inch snow fall during the night. That meant that I would need to use the snow blower before I could take the car out of the garage. The cottage is 10 miles from town, so the car had to be available every day. Almost every morning I was out there opening up the driveway just to get to our road.

Guest Cottage at Brozville during the winter.

Repairs were needed from the very first summer for years to come. That explains why the purchase price was so low. Everything was old and needed repair or replacement. However, we were able to use our home each year, and eventually lived there year round for 10 years. We were able to live there comfortably only after we put a basement under the whole house.

Looking back, we had to rebuild practically the whole place the expensive way: tear it down and rebuild it with new materials. Almost always when tearing down the old, there are unexpected complications which increase the cost. The only new building that I added was an oversized 2 car garage. But after the garage was built is when we started calling the place Brozville. There already was the main cottage, a guest cottage (which was settling into a hole), the wet boat house (that was leaning to the south), and a summer kitchen with screens that were rusting out. The garage was the 5th building and it was starting to look like our own small village.

I had a lot of problems with bears tipping over my garbage almost every night and spilling garbage all over the ground. Of course this had to be picked up by hand. So, in the plans for the garage, I included a small room, 8' by 8', on the front right corner as a place to store my garbage cans. This seemed to be a perfect solution to the bear trouble until one time when I had to leave for one week during the summer. There was garbage in the cans getting ripe for almost two weeks. This would really attracted the bears, even during the daytime. I mean bears.

One day not long after returning, I was home alone and happened to look out the kitchen window where I saw a mother bear and her two small cubs at the door of the garbage room. This was only a hollow core door, and the two cubs had already clawed through the outside panel. Then the mother bear came to the door and put her paw on the door knob. She opened the door, and the cubs were able to get inside with ease. Of course they tipped the cans over and out came the ripe garbage into the back yard. That is part of my exercise program, picking up garbage.

After the basement was added under the main cottage, we were able to be comfortable staying all year. I experienced the real winters in the north for 10 years. The delight of the summers at the lake make up for the struggle of the winters. The summers are a bit short, but we still get beautiful flowers and birds. One extra delight is to see the humming birds come back. They winter in Guatemala and use the jet stream to come back to visit us every year.

Dorothy put a red crystal ornament in the kitchen window. When the humming birds would come back, they would go to the window looking for food. With great delight she would say, "The humming birds are back." Then out comes the feeder which requires special syrup. It has to be made by taking one cup of sugar to one cup of water. and then it has to be heated to make the sugar dissolve. It also has to be stirred while heating. Then two drops of red food coloring give it a red color.

But, this feeder had its own problem, too. The bears were out of the garbage but they like hummingbird syrup, too. The challenge was to keep the bears from tearing the feeder down and drinking the syrup. Yes, the black bears love this stuff and even feed it to their cubs by pouring it into their mouths. The bears roam around at night, and look for any food that is out there. They knock over bird feeders and garbage cans. The story is that was their home first, and we moved in. I outwitted the bears by suspending our feeder on a wire that was attached to our house and then to a tree. This put it above the reach of the bears. Dorothy would keep an eye on it to watch when the feeder needed a refill. She would make the syrup and fill the feeder, but I would hang it up because I was taller.

The cottage is located about 50 miles from Lake Superior and 350 miles from Chicago where I have lived all my life. My first impression was that the neighbors were simply being overly friendly, but we soon learned that there is a dependency on each other. We had to be aware of each others needs as well. It is a true neighborhood where they need to know all about you, including your relatives. It appears that this is necessary here, but also comforting to know that there is someone close by if help is needed. This especially true when all your relatives are hundreds of miles away, and most of the residents are retirees like us.

Ah, summer at the lake. After a brutal winter, the summers are wonderful and pleasant. They call this God's country because after everything is dormant and still for the winter, then everything becomes alive, turns green and grows abundantly. The trees get leaves, and the air is warm and fresh. You can take a deep breath without hurting your chest. Then the final evidence that winter is nearing the end is the breaking up of the ice on the lakes. This can be quite an event especially if it is accompanied with a thunder storm. The cabin is on the eastern shore, and the major storms usually come from the west. The winds bring massive chunks of ice towards our shore, These act like giant bulldozers and push everything out of the way. This could be the reason how our lake got its name, Big Crawling Stone. This ice can move big boulders, piles of rock, dirt, and sand, and even push big logs right over.

When the ice is gone, the water gets warm quickly because it is shallow with a sand bottom. This is wonderful and safe for children, because if they fall, they can stand up quickly on their own. It is really delightful to watch the little ones when they first get in the lake. They smile and laugh and splash the water as if this is a huge bath tub. I have lived long enough to see my third generation go through this, and I still love to watch them. As they get older and learn to swim, they lose the fear of water for the rest of their lives.

The next enjoyment with children growing up is to go fishing and be there when they catch their first fish. After holding a fish pole in the water for a period of time, they feel a jerking of the tip of the pole. Their faces light up, a big grin forms, and with excitement shout, "I caught a fish, I caught a fish!" There is a grandpa story I would like to share with you.

This little grandson comes to his grandfather and asks, "Grandpa can we go fishing?" Grandpa answers, "We could do that, but we have to get ready first." Then he adds, "First we have to get fishing poles, then we have to get the worms from the refrigerator. Now we have go to the boat house to get our life jackets. After we put them on, then we need to get a bucket for the fish. Now we need to get oars for the boat. We also need an anchor in the boat."

After they get everything in the boat, grandpa rows the boat to a likely spot, and he lowers the anchor. He says, "This looks like a good spot. So get your fishing pole, and I will bait the hook. Be careful don't jerk the line, because the hook is very sharp. Now put the line in the water and you are fishing." After a few minutes he catches a fish, and grandpa puts it in the bucket. Then his grandson says," Grandpa, can we go now? I got my fish."

Living at the lake was a new life style for us, especially being on the east shore. There are several advantages, but the major one is the ability to watch the sun setting. I had an opportunity to observe sunrises in the East at different places, but I believe sunsets are better.

There is a serenity and peaceful calmness that occurs in the evening as you sit on the shore watching sunsets. The wind usually becomes calm, and the lake becomes more reflective. Often cloud formations occur creating spectacular color changes that are almost never the same. Generally you get the feeling that you would like to share these periods by getting pictures of them. Dorothy did this often, and every year we had a new supply to give to our relatives and friends.

There is a spiritual nature about watching the sun setting on the horizon that becomes interesting over the course of a year. There is a definite change in the location of the setting sun that can be observed. This leads me to an interesting tradition that might have some truth to it. The Native Americans watched the point of the setting sun intensely. They noticed that when the point of the setting sun was moving to the North, the climate was getting warmer. However when the setting sun was moving south, the climate was getting colder. If the sun continued to move south, their lives would be endangered. If the sun were to continue in that direction, everything would be doomed. All these observations can easily be made by using the tops of the trees on the horizon.

When December 21st comes on our calendar, we call it Winter Solstice, the beginning of our winter. At that time the observers found that it appeared there was no change in the position of the sunset. After a few days it appeared that point of the sunset could be coming back North. After four days, they were sure it was coming back, and they had a celebration. They were happy that the sun was coming back for another summer. When the Christian Missionaries arrived, and told them about our celebration of Christmas. They said that was a day of celebration for them also.

Theologically the native American represents a very interesting and unique group of people. It is my impression that they were removed from all sources of tradition and/or education. Again it is my impression that they had to use their human intellect to survive. I believe that with God's help, they developed their own civilization which included the need for a singular deity. They used the sun to satisfy that need.

They had to start with basics of living which included language and morals. They had to use their human mind to develop all aspects of human life. Some place in my training I had heard that the human mind, left on its own, will find God. In my opinion, I believe that occurred when they found the need for spirituality, and the sun served that purpose. When we first made contact with the Native Americans, there was a form of tapestry called the, "Eye of God." These were large mostly circular pattern, and they were hanging from the ceiling of the church, about 6 or 8, all in different colors and designs. We were given one as a gift. This one is about 3 feet in diameter, and I have another one in my bedroom which is 3 inches in diameter. My interpretation is that these showed that God is watching everywhere and everything. Over the years this custom has disappeared, but we still have ours. The observation that I am trying to show is that the human mind left alone without previous knowledge, will seek and find God, because God does exist. God has that in His design.

For our 25th wedding anniversary, we made a trip to Hawaii. We were island hopping by air from one island to the next in beautiful Hawaii. This is where everyone on the islands wants to get to the mainland, and everyone on the mainland wants to go to the islands. Dorothy and I were alone and were very happy to be able to enjoy all that Hawaii had to offer.

However on leaving one island, with the plane taxiing to take off, there was a loud explosion and a cloud of smoke arose on one side of the plane. The captain was aborting the take-off, and we were all jammed into our seat belts. The plane was able to stop, however, looking out the window, I could see the waves of the ocean. The pilot was able to turn the plane around and taxied back to the hangar. We had blown a tire on take-off. We were told that we all had to leave the plane. Then we were told that that a piece of rubber had lodged into the engine, and we would have to change planes to continue. Some of the passengers were very pale and frightened. Others were taking some pills, perhaps Valium, to relax. We narrowly escaped a serious accident from either the engine exploding and burning or from not having enough runway left to stop. It appears that God has His plan for each of us, and our job on earth was not completed yet. But this was the second time this had happened to us. I believe this was another spiritual happening.

As a doctor, I was in solo practice all my years and thus receive no pension other than Social Security. It wasn't much income, and our finances were getting low. So Dorothy suggested that she might use her nurse's training to find employment. I felt sad but believed this could help. So she checked with a new home health group that was just start-ing up in the area. She talked to them and was told that as a nurse, she would have to be re-licensed, but as a CNA, this would be easier. So she took a refresher course at the local community college, took her exam, and passed with flying colors. She was hired with her new license and continued to work for about five years. She really enjoyed going back and helping patients. Their motto is "Angels on Snow Tires."

This motto is a modern descendant of a service the area had

experienced years ago. In those days, there were very few doctors in the area, but there was one lady doctor that was always available, Dr. Kate. As you know, during the winter in the North woods of Wisconsin, there is plenty of snow, like 3 to 4 feet. Dr. Kate used to make frequent house calls because the patients were unable to get out to see her. So she would take a pair of snow shoes along and use them to walk on the snow if there was no path. The people referred to her as "the Doctor on snow shoes."

So to continue the evolution of the motto, nurses are very often referred to as "angels", and in today's world, the vehicles now have snow tires. Dorothy was able to get a bumper sticker with the new version, and I felt it was very appropriate for us.

However, as happens to all, the years were passing, and Dorothy and I were getting older. She had become quieter and had returned to her old pastime of reading novels. I encouraged her to be more active, even if it meant walking outside. She did some of it, but then she would find another book to read.

As she neared her eightieth birthday, she looked at me and said, "I think I'm losing my mind." She pointed to a window in the kitchen and said, "What is that?" I replied that it was a window, and she said, "Yes, that's right." Our children were planning an eightieth birthday party for her, and I wondered what to do. They planned to have eighty guests for a dinner party and were able to get a restaurant to accommodate our group. Then close to her birthday (which was on June 13th), the party went off beautifully. Seventy-nine guests were present, and Dorothy greeted each one by name at the door as they came in. I was so proud of her. I knew she was developing dementia, and over time, I had to tell our children about their mother's condition.

During our next three years, we had our own apartment in Minocqua, Wisconsin, in a senior living complex. Our number was 303, the same as our condo in Fort Lauderdale, Florida. Those trips to Florida were wonderful, and we were able to have a change of pace. We enjoyed the Florida sun, the beach, the restaurants, and all the warm weather. We flew down frequently--- all pleasant memories now during our stay in #303.

1945 1995

a celebration of love

This was the cover of a booklet given at the Mass on our 50th anniversary.

Over that three year period, Dorothy's dementia seemed to plateau, but it was on a quite severe level. Although she could remember people, she would forget events. She could recite all the prayers at Mass from memory, yet she could not remember how to cook or dress herself.

Dorothy with great grandchildren and Cathy, who is grandson's Frank's wife.

St. Anthony Church in Lac du Flambeau, WI with
Father John about 1990. Dorothy is in the center.

One day she woke up with some redness in her left ear, which I did not think was important. However the next day, her ear and part of left cheek were red and swollen. I put an antibiotic crème on it, but on the third day, it had spread to the entire left side of her face. I placed an urgent call to her doctor who said to bring her right in. After seeing her, he said that she would have to be hospitalized for intravenous antibiotics. The next morning in the hospital, the

Family reunion on Dorothy's 80th birthday party.

Dorothy's 80th birthday party with all our children, from left, Jack, Rick, Bob, Gary, Roger, Ray, in front, Sue, me, Dorothy, Barb.

infection had spread to her forehead, and she appeared confused. When I arrived, the night nurse told me that Dorothy had gone to the bathroom during the night and pulled out the IV needle. She had dripped blood in the bathroom, on the floor, on herself, and on the bed. The nurse scolded her, but it appeared that Dorothy did not comprehend what the nurse was talking about. The next day Dorothy asked the nurse, "Is this a hospital?" The nurse told her, "Yes, and you are in it." Finally the medication worked, and the infection cleared. Dorothy left the hospital after eleven days, and we returned to our apartment.

After I would get things under control at the apartment, and Dorothy was settled, I would make a tripe to Brozville almost daily. I continued to have a vegetable garden there, and to visit with any guests that would be vacationing there. It is very popular with my large family. On one of those visits an unusual event happened. I want to present this as a story.

Not everyone has the key to a Chevy mounted in a frame. In fact I think I might be the only person who owns such a thing, especially because the truck it belongs to, isn't even mine. How this key came

Dorothy and me on our balcony in our apartment in Minocqua, Wisconsin.

into my possession is a story and a half. My granddaughter, Rachel, and her family, including Jan, her mother in law, came to the cabin over the Fourth of July weekend in 2007. As the weekend drew to a close, everyone was packing and getting ready for the drive home. Rachel was doing the packing for her kids and Kris, her husband, was moving bags and suitcases around. Jan decided to move her truck a bit closer to the cabin to facilitate the packing process.

First Miracle to happen to us at Brozville.

After a short while, I noticed Rachel, Kris, and Jan standing around Jan's truck, peering into the windows and looking dismayed. I came outside to investigate, and they told me that Jan had inadvertently left her keys in the ignition of the truck, and then locked the doors out of habit with the keys hanging in the ignition, and the engine turned off. We began considering the options. It was nearly 6:00 PM on the last day of a holiday weekend, so our options were severely limited. Locksmiths were closed for the holidays, the nearest car dealership that could make a new key for the truck was over ten miles away, and they were also closed for the holiday weekend. We were running out of time and ideas, short of smashing the car window. Jan had to get back to the Twin Cities for work the next day, and no one wanted to break the window. Kris stared at the ground, looking for anything that might trigger a perfect solution to this dire situation.

All of a sudden, his eyes drifted over a spot on the sand and immediately snapped back to where they'd been a second before." What's this?" he said, and as he pointed to a bright speck on the ground, he was already moving toward it. Immediately next to the rear left tire of the truck was a new-looking Chevrolet car key. He picked it up. It was unadorned with a key chain or other decoration. Everyone swore they'd never seen it before, and we'd been standing around for over thirty minutes, trying to find a way into the truck. Jan didn't recognize it and said it wasn't hers. No one else present drove a Chevy. There wasn't any way for the key to be on the ground, but nevertheless, there it was now in Kris's hand. I told him to try it in the door. After all, if it didn't work, we wouldn't be any worse off than we already were.

Kris stuck the key in the door lock and surprisingly, it slid right in, but we were heartbroken to find out that it wouldn't turn in the lock. More out of frustration than anything else, I told him to try it on the passenger side door. He looked at me skeptically and walked around the truck to try it, knowing that it wouldn't work.

Like the driver's door, the key went in, but this time, when Kris gave it a twist, the door unlocked. We all stood in the yard staring at each other and at the truck, then at the key. I don't remember who talked first or what they said, but everyone knew that what had just happened was beyond rational explanation. I know that the Lord works in mysterious ways, but that day, He gave us a key to a locked car and everyone was able to return home according to plan. Jan agreed; the key was put there by a higher power. She gave me the key as a reminder of what we had witnessed that July afternoon, and that's why I have the key to a Chevy mounted in a frame.

I continued to take care for Dorothy, but there was no improvement in her dementia. Then one morning, she told me she couldn't find her teeth. She had an upper partial that was not very large but included some front teeth. We looked under the covers, under the bed, in the bathroom, on the floor, but we could not find them anywhere. Yet believing that they were in the apartment, and that they would show up, we thought we would just wait and hope. She was able to eat without the partial, so it wasn't that urgent.

After about two weeks and no partial, we decided that she will need a replacement. Off we went to the dentist where she had to have all her teeth examined including X-rays. Then she needed one tiny filling. She'd gone nearly one month without her partial and was ready for the impression. It was made, and, would you believe, that very night we found her teeth. They were in the far end of her pillowcase. The dentist was very kind and did not charge us for the impression.

We reached the point where I had to do everything for her, the shopping, the cooking, the cleaning, the bathing, but I still had time to read my newspaper. She could watch television, but I had to read the newspaper to her. Her hearing was quite good while mine isn't. I found some humor in the fact that when we were young, I would enjoy undressing her, but now, in our old age, I have to dress her every day. She would try to dress herself on occasion but would always get her clothes on backward. She would get very frustrated when I would tell her that she would have to take them off and turn them around. One day I missed, and she was at the hair dresser who told her, "Dorothy, you have your top on backward."

Morning time in our apartment in Minocqua Wis. About 2007.

Winter view from our 3rd floor balcony with clearing the parking area.

# Chapter 8: Illness and Death

On March 5, 2008, at 2:00 AM, I awoke to the sound of Dorothy screaming, "I fell on the floor! I can't move!" I got out of bed and found her lying on the floor in the bedroom doorway, complaining that she could not move her legs. I tried moving her right leg, and she screamed that it hurt. I palpated over her right hip, and she said, "Yes that hurts, I fell backward and hit my head."

I suspected that she had broken her hip, so I called 911 for an ambulance. I had to wait, but they came at 2:30. I informed them that she has a broken right hip. They carefully rolled her onto a stretcher and put her in the ambulance. After about another 30 minutes they got on the road. Finally we got to the emergency room, and then there was more waiting for me in the lobby. All the admission testing and x-rays had to be taken.

Finally I was able to talk to the emergency room doctor. He confirmed that she had a broken right hip and said that she had to be admitted to the hospital. He also had called an orthopedic surgeon who would see her in the morning. After all of this was finished, I returned to our apartment at 6:00 AM. I waited until 6:30 AM to call my son in Eden Prairie, Minnesota to inform him of what had happened to his mother. He said that he and his wife would come as soon as possible. I explained that Dorothy was in no immediate danger. Surgery was scheduled for the next day when her right hip was to be pinned.

After the surgery, the surgeon explained that everything had gone well but that the end of the pin was a little close to the joint. Also that she would be unable to put any weight on the right leg for eight weeks. This meant that she would be in a nursing home for that period of time. She would not be able to walk and would be getting physical therapy daily to keep both upper and lower extremities mobile.

Dorothy was very sad and kept asking me to take her home. But I had to tell her that I couldn't do that because she had a broken hip. She looked at me in disbelief and I realized that she couldn't comprehend the fact that she had any thing broken. Shortly after she was hospitalized, our very kind pastor came to see her and visited her almost daily. He came frequently to the nursing home, even though it was about twelve miles from his residence. He heard her last confession, anointed her with oils, and he prayed over and with her. He also brought her communion every time he came, sensing perhaps that this might be her last illness. My family was urging me to have Dorothy moved to Minnesota because of the long distance they had to travel to visit her. My daughter, Barbara, is a social worker in Minnesota, and a lot of our family also live there. I talked to Dorothy's doctor who said that the only way to accomplish that was to go from one nursing home to another.

Dorothy was not doing well in physical therapy. The therapists were yelling at her, and she would say, "I can't do it." After the eight week period they tried to make her put weight on her right leg. I believe she could not tell them that it hurt too much. It seemed like they could not understand that she was also a dementia patient. The nursing home staff reported her to the insurance company as making no progress, and immediately her insurance was cancelled. I wasn't informed of this until about a week later when the nursing home handed me a bill for $6,000.00.

During that time we found a nursing home in Minnesota that would accept her as a patient. We were able to secure a medical van that would be able to take her to Minnesota. We scheduled to move her on May 13th at 7:00 AM. The driver put her on a stretcher and fastened it to the floor. I rode in the front seat, and off we went. The weather was great, and in four hours we reached the Minnesota nursing home. Dorothy withstood the trip pretty well except for the last hour when she became very frightened. She could not understand what was happening.

At the new nursing home, because of her dementia, she was put on a dementia floor in spite of the hip fracture. Normally she would be on a surgical floor with a hip fracture. The next day we went to the new orthopedic surgeon for examination and orders. They took more x-rays, and he informed us that the pin had shifted and was very likely in the hip joint causing the extreme pain. Then he looked at Dorothy and said, "You don't want another surgery, do you?" She didn't reply, and again I believe she didn't understand what was going on. She never told him she was having any pain. He went on to say that he wanted to see her in two weeks. She was seated comfortably in a wheelchair. We returned to her room in the new nursing home which was so much better than the one in Wisconsin, which was an old hospital building converted into a nursing home.

This was a newer building, and it was built as a nursing home. Also the personnel were more helpful and very pleasant. Everything looked bright and cheerful, but Dorothy didn't want to live this way any longer. Her mind was starting to function in a strange way. She was scheming ways to die. Even though all during this time she knew all of us, and recognized us by name, she had a death wish. She told me to wheel her wheelchair over to the stairway and push her over. I told her that I couldn't do that. She also told our daughter-in-law to take her to the street and push her wheelchair into the traffic. She was trying to see if I would not help her, maybe someone else would.

Previously, while we were in our apartment, Dorothy felt sad about her mental problems. She told me to help her to go over the railing on our balcony, because we lived on the third floor. She said that she wanted to go, so I could go on with my life. I would casually respond by telling her not to talk that way. This reminded me of when Dorothy's mother was in her last years and would say, "I'm ready to go now." Dorothy was trying to show compassion for me. When she was transferred to the last nursing home, she was more alert than most of the other Alzheimer patients that were there. She told me, "I know I am a little crazy, but these people are really crazy." This was the reason I felt her dementia was not true Alzheimer's. I believe she had Senile Dementia where some parts of the brain are not impaired while other parts are involved.

She recognized us by name. I could talk to her about specific members of the family, and she knew who I was talking about. Occasionally, she would even correct me if I used the wrong child's name in a particular family. When her eighty-fifth birthday was approaching, our daughter Barbara, organized a little party for her on her floor. All the floor personnel on her floor were very supportive of having the family come for a little celebration. Our granddaughter, Rachel, came with her husband and our three great-grandchildren. Also there was our son Jack and his wife, and Barbara and I. We had decorated tables with flowers and cake and candy. A nice group, and a nice party, and we all sang, "Happy Birthday" to Dorothy, who was smiling most of the time. It was a festive time. Dorothy had her birthday party on Saturday, June 7th.

Dorothy's last photo at her 85th birthday party with Granddaughter Rachel's family and me.

On Monday June 9th at 6:00 AM, Dorothy went into shock. She developed a rapid pulse, a fall in blood pressure, and had emesis. The nurses called 911 for an ambulance to take her to the emergency room at the hospital. Then they called our daughter, Barbara, to inform the family. When we arrived, all the monitors were attached and the IVs were running. Barbara was at her bedside and Dorothy put on a little smile when she saw us. They had already taken a chest x- ray, and the report would arrive shortly. She told me softly, "Please let me go." I could not answer her, because I felt she knew she was dying. Her condition was not improving as we waited in the room. When the x-ray report arrived, we were told that there were blood clots in both lungs, a very ominous report.

As we were getting older, She and I would talk about death and dying, which usually occurred when we renewed our driver's licenses. They would ask us if we wanted an organ donor sticker on our license, and we talked about a living will. This would preclude any extraordinary efforts to be made on our behalf to prolong our life. This would apply especially if a ventilator tube had to be inserted in the throat. So we both felt that at our age, we didn't want this to be done.

To have a living will prepared properly, we went to our attorney friend who drew up the appropriate papers before the need arose. It appeared that this might be the time when a decision like that might have to be made. My daughter, Barbara, was well aware of our feelings.

Eventually the emergency room physician arrived and took me aside for a conference. He said that Dorothy had a very rapid pulse but she also had very low blood pressure. If he gave her medication to slow down her pulse, it would also reduce her blood pressure further. Conversely, if he used medication to raise her blood pressure, it would increase her pulse rate. I remembered our living will that stated that we did not want extraordinary measures to prevent dying. Knowing Dorothy's desires, I asked him to just make her comfortable.

When I returned to her bedside, she looked at me with sadness in her eyes, and she knew who I was. With her eyes wide open, she said almost as a command, "Let me go." I did not say a word. I was speechless, because that was just what I told her doctor to do. I reach over and held her hand. The nurse arrived and put some medication in her IV, which helped her relax. She was able to close her eyes and rest. About an hour later, her body went limp, and the monitors became erratic. Dorothy DIED. She went to her Heavenly Father. Every one in the room was crying, but I was sobbing, the hardest crying I had ever done in my life. Her life on earth was finished, and she got her wish to go. We all cried for about 30 minutes. My grief has been profound, but I will accept God's will.

Lying in her casket, she was as beautiful as ever. Her great-grandchildren who had attended her last party said to their mother, "Grandma has a smile on her face." I saw that there was a small smile on her face as if to tell people that her soul was in a happy place. No more pain and suffering for her. Her body was broken, and her soul had left for a new place prepared for her by her Heavenly Father. Sometime ago, she had told me that she would see me in Heaven. On June 9th , the day she died, was also our sixty-third wedding anniversary. June 13, the day of her burial, was also her eighty-fifth birthday. I felt that the greatest gift I could give to her was peace and rest with her Lord. To me, it seemed that our Heavenly Father had planned it that way.

# Chapter 9: Miracles

The day of her funeral, our son Rick looked out of his kitchen window and saw two deer in his back yard. It is very unusual to see deer there in the morning, and an old Native American tradition says that God will send animals to console you when you lose a loved one. Also I learned later that my grandson's wife, Cathy, looked out her West window on the evening of Dorothy's death, and she saw a beautiful sun set. She was so impressed that she got her camera and took a picture of it. She was not aware of Dorothy's death at that time.

About a week later, while I was living in my son's home in Eden Prairie, Minnesota, I was in the back yard when I saw an eagle soaring overhead. This is a very unusual sight for Eden Prairie. The eagle had come from the north and was traveling eastward. As if it spotted me, the eagle made a U turn and flew directly over my head.

One month later, on July 8, I was working outside at the lake home in Lac du Flambeau. I was all alone, and it was a hot day. I was picking up some split logs and putting them in a cart. When I was almost finished, I heard a voice say, "That's enough already." It sounded like Dorothy's voice but I looked around and saw no one. Thinking it was my imagination, I ignored it and continued picking up the last few logs. Again I heard her voice say, "That's enough already!" That time I was sure it was Dorothy's voice, and not my imagination, so I ended the job by sweeping the rest into the forest.

When I told a very dear friend of mine, Sister Teresa, what had happened, she said that in Aramaic, Jesus' language, heaven is translated as, "Eagles and voices." I had experienced both. I am sure that Dorothy is in heaven.

Since her death, we have experienced several other spiritual events in the family. Four days later, on July 12, we had a family reunion that had been scheduled about a year before. A large group was attending, including my grandson, Paul, and his wife, Kate. During the night, Kate had a dream in which she actually saw Dorothy clearly with glowing, white radiant hair. She spoke to Kate, saying, "Tell Paul this place is not the same," and the dream ended. I believe that the meaning behind that statement was that Dorothy and I gave the property to our son, Jack, who subsequently made some changes. To me these spiritual events seems to prove that Dorothy is in heaven and is still able to communicate with us.

The wedding of Paul and Kate, the parents of Atlas Broz. (left to right) Dorothy, me, Grandma Kobor, Paul, Kate, Grandpa Tyrrell and Grandpa Hoffman.

Rick's entire family in 2003 at his son, Paul's wedding.

Later in that year in November, Paul and Kate had a little son, Atlas James, who is now about two months old. He was not gaining weight, and it appeared that he was not able to retain his feedings. It was possible that he was suffering from hypertrophic pyloric stenosis. When I saw him, I felt he was a very sick little boy. He was hospitalized and was scheduled for surgery the next morning. I felt very sad, and then I prayed to Dorothy if she could help Atlas, our great grandson. That evening the doctors declared him **CURED**. He was able to retain his feedings. The next morning the surgery was cancelled, and he went home instead. He gained three pounds the next month.

Several years ago, it's hard to pinpoint the time, we were visiting my grandmother, Grandma Bilek. It was a special event, because all of our eight children were along. When she saw our family for the first time, she was surprised and she said, "These children are your stairway to heaven." Her prophecy was fulfilled when Dorothy died.

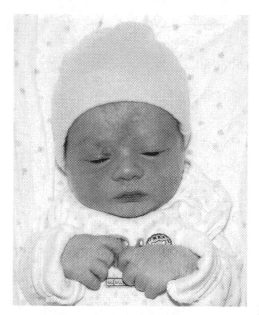

Newborn Atlas Broz son of Paul and Kate who was **CURED** before surgery at 2 months of age through Dorothy's intercession.

Same Atlas Broz about 1 year of age.

When all these spiritual events happen to our family, I feel that Dorothy is asking God to send us these blessings. However I believe that God has a plan for all of us and when such events happen to us, we should be very thankful. We should say, "Thank you," to our heavenly Father who is kind and generous.

I wish to close with a quote from the prophet Jeremiah (29:11) "For surely I know the plans I have for you," says the Lord, "Plans for your welfare and not for harm, to give you a future with hope." Amen.

# Chapter 10: Eulogy

## The Hummingbirds Have Gone – Margaret Broz

Shakespeare said, "Give sorrow words." These are a few thoughts I've had about my grandmother's recent passing. She was quiet, yet strong. She raised eight sons and daughters and welcomed each new addition they brought to the Broz clan. When her children had grown, she dedicated her life to continuing to care for children and others at her church and on the reservation. Her heart was so full of love and life that everyone around her benefited from knowing her. She had a twinkle in her eyes as if she knew a wonderful, joyous secret, and if you listened hard and were patient enough, she'd help you know it, too.

I remember quiet times in the kitchen and stories told in a soft, quiet voice. There was a mischievous side to her, too. It would sneak out as a wry comment or a quick wink, and even on the last day I saw her, she was feisty, cheerful, and giving Grandpa a hard time. I was overjoyed that she was in such good spirits and that I was able to share that time with her and my family. She was the one who inspired me to learn embroidery. The stitching she made for me that celebrated my birth has hung in my bedroom since before I can remember and now hangs in my living room. I am so very grateful that

I got the chance to give her the embroidery I made of the anniversary family tree. I remember, as I handed it to her, that she looked at the front, then turned it over for a quick look at the back. To my chagrin, it was a plain backing and I apologized for not signing it. She said, "Oh, that's okay. I always look at the back," and smiled.

I remember the richly decorated cottages, not rich in the monetary sense but in a rustic, homey, lived-in and loved-in way. The jolly stuffed witch dolls above the sink, the photo board in the kitchen with pictures of grandkids; humorous, tender, and devout plaques on the walls; the cheeky "Chipmunk Crossing" sign by the big cottage; the intricate embroideries, paintings, and native decorations, even the window decals of birds' shadows so none would fly into the picture window. And of course, the hummingbird feeder just outside the kitchen window. I remember fried blue gills from the lake. We would start the day hunting for minnows with the big square net. If we weren't successful, there was always the trusty plastic container of worms.

Then we'd fish all day off the pier, triumphantly placing each fish into the bucket until it was time to clean them. Dad would clean them (I stayed away, not wanting to witness the grossness!) and would leave the boathouse with that unique smell, which now has come to be very comforting to me. Then we'd take the fish up the hill to Grandma who would bread them and fry them up for dinner. I don't know how she managed to make them so delicious, but they're one of my fondest memories of meals in Minocqua. I remember sunny days of swimming, stormy days of playing games, and the absence of TV that helped us spend our vacation time bonding as a family and enjoying the wonders of nature. I remember big soft towels and sleeping in bunks near my siblings, each night like another slumber party. I remember expansive family meals and the pervasive sense of warmth and love everywhere.

And behind it all was Grandma. So serene and calm, her caring nature pervaded everything. Minocqua represents everything good and peaceful in my life. Grandma has passed on, but I still feel her there. The hummingbird feeders are gone, but I know she has guided them on to other food, even now caring for the creatures of this earth.